Conway Lloyd Morgan

SPERONE

PHOTOGRAPHS
by Richard Bryant

This book would not have been possible without the enthusiastic support of Guy and Jacques Dewez: indeed without their enthusiasm, tenacity and judgement over three decades, Sperone itself would never have been achieved. The owners of the individual properties made us welcome, contributing their own texts and ideas, and sharing their love of the place. Special thanks go to Bruno Allais for his wry but stern comments on the planning and building actualities of the development, and to the architects of GEA, André, Breton, Brzeczkowski and Roques , for their unflagging interest and attention to detail. Working with Richard Bryant has been both enriching and enjoyable: his artistry and dedication make the most important contribution to this book. It has been a pleasure and a privilege for me to work as part of such a team.

Adès S.A.
(Société nouvelle Adam Biro, 28, rue de Sévigné, 75004 Paris)
ISBN : 2-87660-191-5

Collaborators: Jacqui Visick, Douglas Finney.

Editorial coordination: Marlyne Kherlakian.
Layout: Sophie Zagradsky.
Copy editing: Lisa Davidson, Elizabeth Ayre.

CONTENTS

Louis Bériot is a journalist and television producer and has written several novels and essays. He co-produced the television programme *La France défigurée*, broadcast from 1971 to 1977 on the first channel, and is highly experienced in the fields of urban planning and environmental issues. After producing numerous broadcasts for France Inter, Europe 1 and Antenne 2, he became a consultant to the President of France Télévision and Director of France 2. He returned to writing in the summer of 1996.

THE SPERONE DOMAIN: A MODEL DEVELOPMENT

Sperone, Falatte, Ciappili, Piantarella—these sites all encompass the millenia of struggle between the violence and torment of nature and the tenacity and intrepidity of man.

A turbulent alliance was born of this combat, an alliance constantly redefined by man's occupation of the site and threatened by the wear and tear of time and nature.

Some twenty centuries ago, the Romans founded a port between Sperone and Piantarella, where they constructed a town and started trading in the age-old stones from the Cavallo Island.

Today, all that remains of the port is a memory; and of the city, a few ruins. Yet the Romans pursued and appreciated beauty—the lagoon that sheltered the boats between two spurs of limestone overgrown by the *maquis* has become a magical haven for thousands of migratory and sedentary birds.

Nature, once again, has triumphed.

The epic of Sperone and Piantarella inspired Guy and Jacques Dewez, the designers of the real-estate development constructed on this site.

The presence of man on a natural site is, of course, always problematic. Extreme care must be taken so that it does not become an irremediable intrusion. There are several possibilities. In one, the amenities, housing, plants, maquis and rocks meld together into a unique, yet harmonious, whole. In the other, when the site itself is disrupted and cannot be recreated, the wound is irreversible and irreparable.

The promoters wanted to move into the Sperone domain as friends, not intruders, and to create a project that would coincide with their principles.

The decision to use wood, a renewable resource; the architectural designs of homes that fit into, rather than impose themselves into the landscape; and the design of the golf course, which incorporates the *maquis*, all reflect the care and tact guiding the conception of this development.

We can now see the results. The Sperone domain is famous throughout the world as a model of integrated architecture, and its golf course is considered to be one of the five most beautiful in Europe.

LOUIS BÉRIOT

INTRODUCTION

The first image taken by the French satellite GéoSpot in 1993 was of the south-east tip of Corsica and the northern tip of Sardinia. (DR)

"The harbour at Bonifacio offers good shelter in deep water" is the matter-of-fact description in the *Western Mediterranean Pilot.* In fact this port, at the southern end of the island, is one of the finest natural harbours in the Mediterranean; protected by steep cliffs on either side, the narrow entrance is accessible under most weather conditions. It is a safe haven, but also an easily defended one—for centuries after the Romans left the island, Mediterranean pirates used Bonifacio as a base.

Bonifacio was named after a Tuscan prince, Bonifacio di Toscana, who, so the story goes, founded the city in 828, though it is more likely that he lent his name to an existing town. Three centuries later, the Genoese, from one of the most powerful mercantile cities of Italy, were fighting to control Corsica. A glance at the map shows why such a relatively poor island was so important—Corsica controls the entrance to the Ligurian Sea, on which Genoa sits. Not only were pirates operating from the island (Porto Vecchio was still a pirate's haven in the sixteenth century), but Corsica could not be allowed to fall into the hands of Genoa's great maritime rivals, Pisa or Venice.

The island supplied timber and pitch for Genoa's growing merchant fleet, but the main reason they occupied the island was not primarily mercantile but strategic. The Genoese settled primarily along the coast, by developing existing facilities or building new ports. The present map of the island reflects the importance of coastal towns over those in the interior. The old town of Bonifacio was fortified under Genoese rule, and a bastion wall and corner tower were constructed along the southern cliff, some 500 feet above the harbour. The Genoese settled their colonists in the new towns, and until recently, some Bonifaciens even used the term "Bonifacio proprio" to distinguish themselves from other Corsicans. Although other colonization attempts failed—due to local resistance and the endemic malaria—the Genoese generally improved the economy and agriculture of Corsica.

The port of Bonifacio in the late 1960s

The Genoese remained in Corsica for over six hundred years, finally ceding the island to France in 1768 under the Treaty of Versailles. (It is thus a quirk of history that Napoleon Bonaparte's elder brother was born under Italian rule; Napoleon himself, Corsica's most famous son, was born under French rule.) The frequency of Italian place names and family names is a continuing reminder of the years of Genoese control of the island.

The French established a series of military and naval posts along the coast, linked by semaphore stations and lighthouses, and later, stationed the Foreign Legion on the island. But the change of political status made little difference in Corsica, where agriculture (particularly sheep rearing), and fishing remained the main industries until this century.

Corsica may be the fourth largest of the Mediterranean islands, but it has always been underpopulated: the neighbouring island of

Granite coastline of
Sperone

The cliffs of Bonifacio

The *maquis* in the evening light

Sardinia is three times larger, but supports seven times the population of Corsica. There are few large settlements in the interior of the island—most of the towns are coastal ports.

The hard life of Corsican seamen is recounted in some of Alphonse Daudet's stories, which contrast the wild sea and harsh *maquis* of southern Corsica with the relative plenty of his beloved Provence. The proud and independent spirit of the Corsicans, a truly Mediterranean people, nonetheless earned his respect. The reputation of Corsica as a strange, wild and beautiful place was further fostered by Prosper Merimée's writings.

In the same way that many Italians regard the adjacent island of Sicily as somehow not quite part of their country, Corsica, as near geographically to Italy as it is to France, has always found itself ambiguously placed on the southern extreme of mainland France.

In the first half of the twentieth century, Corsica's population dropped slowly, mainly due to emigration. An influx of settlers from Algeria (Pieds-Noirs) boosted the population, but their arrival led to a resurgence of nationalist feelings in Corsica. Nonetheless, Corsica is more prosperous now than it was two decades ago, and the provision of infrastructure and social facilities is immeasurably better. But in many ways Corsica remains "the closest of the far-off islands", and in that mystery lies much of the island's powerful charm.

South-east of Bonifacio lie the Straits of Bonifacio. They are dotted with a pattern of islands, and separate Corsica from Sardinia, 8 nautical miles away. On the Corsican side, walls of chalk weathered and eroded by the sea into fantastic shapes show a hint of the inland *maquis* at the cliff top. Below, a few inlets offer approaches to the land. At one of these, just beyond Cape Pertusato, are the remains of a Roman military post. Overlooking the straits, it guarded the Roman Empire's prison quarries on the Lavezzi Islands. For the modern sailor, the play of wind and currents in the straits offers an exciting challenge. Above all, the setting is one of great natural beauty, with the whites and greys of the cliffs leading into the greens and greys of the *maquis*. Corsica is mainly formed of granite, but around Bonifacio a superposed stratum of chalk appears on the surface, creating a different, lighter landscape than the harder, greyer northern part of the island. The sea itself in the Straits of Bonifacio shows an astonishing range of colours, from bleached turquoise to deep blue.

The inland routes from Bonifacio, along the coast, are equally spectacular as the road rises through the chalk cliffs to the main plateau. Here, a further contrast appears between the few areas with a natural water supply and the pervading dry *maquis*. The road winds along headlands and inlets, offering glimpses of the blue sea below, and some of the history of the island unfolds with old semaphore towers, an empty lighthouse, and an abandoned fort, presumably designed by the Foreign Legion in the best Beau Geste tradition. The local dry-stone walls in pale grey granite stand out against the dark green scrub of dwarf pine, wild myrtle and thorn bushes that hug the rough grass. One coastal road runs to the Pointe de Sperone. This small cape forms the southernmost tip of the island; from here, the coast runs westwards to Cape Pertusato and north-eastwards to the Punta di Capicciolo. The Sperone domain runs as far as Ciappili to the west and Piantarella in the east, along a series of promontories looking over the sea towards the islands of Piana and Cavallo and the Lavezzi archipelago. It covers a total area of 325 acres. For many years the family that owned the land kept it as a farm, grazing sheep on the hilltops and growing olives on the slopes. The overall colour of the landscape was the grey and green of the rough *maquis*, with outcrops of white chalk and grey granite.

Imagine arriving from the sea. The cliffs, sea and *maquis* are still there, but in the valley of Ciappili and on the promontories of the

Ciappili and the semaphore station.
Below: view of the Pointe de Sperone

The Ferreri house

Roof of the Ferreri house

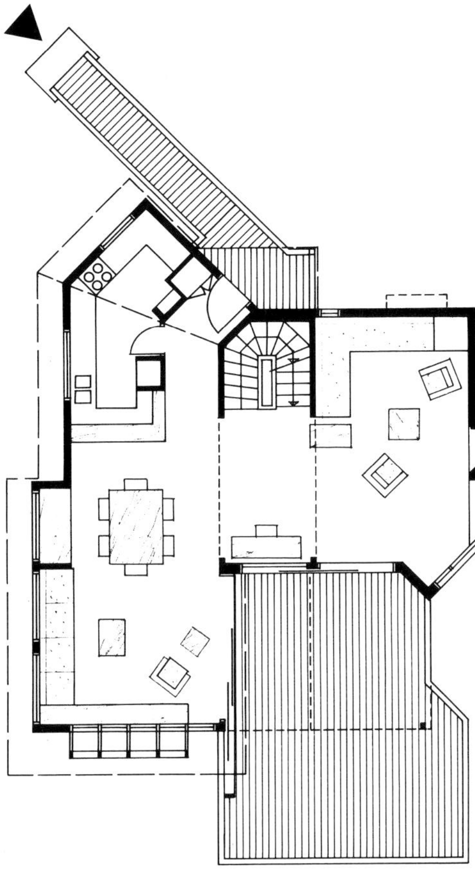

Main level

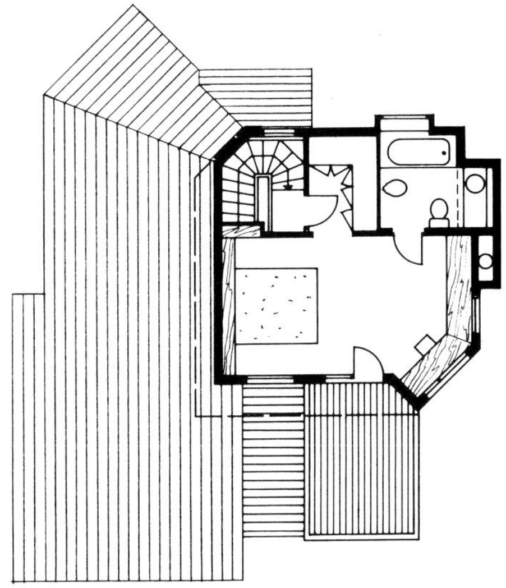

Upper level

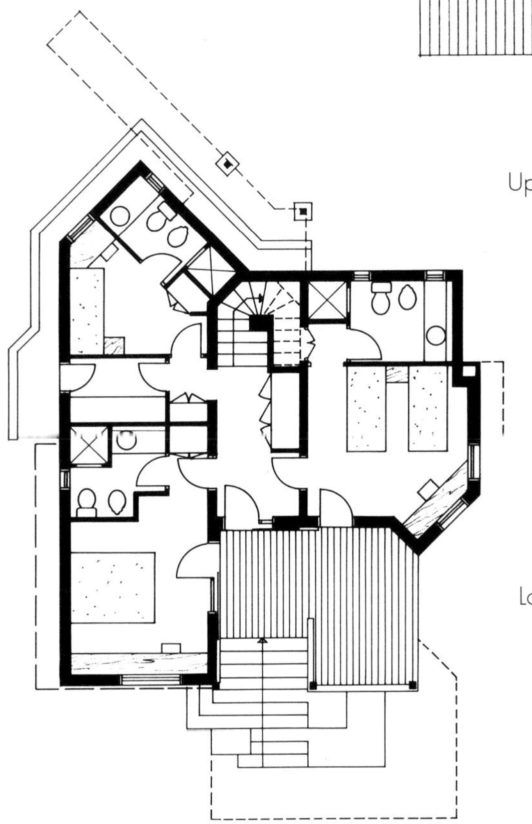

Lower level

Floor plans of the Ferreri house. Architects: GEA

Living room of the Ferreri
house

The master bedroom

The Ferreri house: façade
detail

Hauts de Sperone and Falatte, angular wooden shapes—the profiles of the houses on the domain—come into view. Almost all of the houses are in wood, most unpainted, the wood left to weather naturally into the same silvery, dark tones as the surrounding landscape. One such house is the Ferreri house, which looks down the slope of Ciappili and out to sea.

Seen from the seaward side, the house in elevation resembles a right-angled triangle, with the shortest side as the vertical. The two sloping roofs match the slope on the valley, as if the house had grown there, rather than been built. Depending on the angle at which the bright sunlight falls, the wooden shuttering and roof tiles appear to be either grey or brown, sometimes even black. Even from a distance, it is clear that the doors and large windows are set back beneath the roof overhang, and open onto balconies and decks lined with wooden railings. Behind and around the house, other houses appear through the trees and bushes—all share the same irregular, natural forms, all are part of the landscape, not a burden on it.

From close up, it is clear that the house is on three levels, not the two that are visible above the trees. As the house is set on a slope, there is, as the plans show, a second entrance on the landward side, reached by a wooden walkway to the first floor level. The ground floor, oddly enough, is a bedroom level, and the main living area is on the first floor, with a master bedroom on the top floor. A single tight staircase links all three levels. In the main living area, the emphasis of the design is on access: the kitchen area at the back of the house opens into the living area occupying the rest of the floor through an open breakfast bar, and the living area beside the kitchen gives onto the adjoining deck through sliding glass doors that run back into the frame of the deck, creating a completely open space. Only around the fireplace, at the other side of the living area, is there any sense of enclosure.

On the lower bedroom level, the two double bedrooms each have two sets of entry doors, one into the staircase hall, the other onto the open deck. Similarly, the main parts of the living area above can be reached either via the hallway or the deck. Each deck is in turn shaded by the one above, and that on the top floor by an open latticework. One rapidly realizes that the decks are the central features linking the elements of the house. A traditional house is designed to separate interior from exterior, and staircases, hall and landings are used to articulate the interior spaces. Here the staircase is less prominent, and the distinction between interior and exterior blurs; the decks—simple planked platforms facing the sun, the sea air and the scents of the *maquis*—form the real heart of the house.

This novel arrangement also explains the inversion of the floor arrangements: the guest rooms are on the lower level, because that is the coolest and shadiest area, and the living area is above the level of the trees, to benefit from the light and the view. The arrangement of the rooms around the decks is also unusual. Because the house was designed to interfere as little as possible with the site and its vegetation, a rectilinear plan could not be imposed. The house follows the contours of the site, both in plan and elevation, taking advantage of the slope, as has been seen, to provide a second entrance. The rooms radiate from the centre, their passage marked by changing roof lines. This creates a freedom to use unusual room plans, providing, for example, different views from windows on each level, particularly at the back of the house. Combined with the upward movement of the house into the sunlight and air, this radial disposition creates a helicoidal structure, rich in internal spaces and angles.

The fact that wood is the building material used for this house (and, as will be seen, for most of the others at Sperone) not only coincides with the idea of not imposing the buildings on their site, but also allows a greater variety of floor plans and structures than might be possible with more conventional materials.

In the foreground, the roof of the Ferreri house. To the left, the Ikam house

Façade of the Ferreri
house facing the sea.
In the background, one
of the first houses
at Ciappili

Wood offers the architect flexibility and freedom of choice, like an Erector set that can be constructed in myriad ways. It is also an integrating element: wooden floors run seamlessly from interior to exterior and the structures themselves are sufficiently light to allow them to move slightly with the passage of the wind. Without ever creating an impression of danger, the building seems to be a living thing, especially where, as with the Ferreri house, the surrounding vegetation, both wild and in the garden, has grown up around and even over the house. The bougainvillaea that covers the landward corner of the house not only provides a brilliant touch of colour but also links the balustrades, frames and woodwork of the house with the surrounding greenery.

The Ferreri house is quite small, with only six rooms in all. It is constructed from the simplest of materials, and furnished with elegance but without fuss. But behind this simplicity of appearance lies a complex architectural solution to a keen problem: how to create a form that will live with its environment, not in opposition to it, and allow those living there to enjoy the natural beauty around them in a calm and civilized way. The Ferreri house was not one of the first to be built at Sperone. It emerged, in fact, from an architectural approach to the site that began twenty years before the house was built. To understand Sperone, we need to start at the beginning of the venture. This story forms the next chapter, before examining in more detail some of the houses that have been built. It then looks at the future development of the whole site and its implications as a model of Mediterranean architecture.

HOW SPERONE WAS CREATED AND DEVELOPED

The Dewez brother–Jacques and Guy–in front of a house at Ciappili in 1973 (Cover of *The Daily Telegraph Magazine*)

In 1973, *The Daily Telegraph Magazine* presented Guy and Jacques Dewez, and their plans for the development of Sperone:

It seems probable that the southern tip of Corsica would not now be in process of transformation into a rather special holiday region if, in the high summer of 1962, two brothers—one French, one English—had not finally decided that they could no longer endure the widespread overdevelopment in southern France, particularly St Tropez. Those milling quays. Those cheek-to-cheek beaches. Those yachts packed like sardines.

Jacques Dewez, 46, the Frenchman, and his brother Guy Dewez, 56, who had been born in London and had later opted for British nationality—both of them dedicated yachtsmen—decided to sell up their property on the Côte d'Azur, and find somewhere where it would be possible once more to enjoy the sea in peace.

Some months later the Dewez brothers, snatching a brief holiday away from their businesses in Paris—Guy was then in banking, Jacques in property management—found themselves driving around the far south-east of Corsica, and savouring what they saw.

The scene was the opposite of the Côte d'Azur. Mile upon mile of empty silver-sand beaches, without a bikini or a camper in sight. Above the beaches, thousands of acres of scented "*maquis*", a dense shrub-carpet of wild myrtle and thyme and rosemary. And, most auspicious of all, a sea round this coast and narrow straits dividing this tip of Corsica from Sardinia, that were ideal for yachtsmen.

But where would the yachts go in the winter-time and, indeed, whenever they needed servicing? There was, as the Dewez brothers had long been aware, a naval-cum-fishing-cum-yachting harbour in Bonifacio, the largest town in the district. Now, they drove over to take a fresh look at it.

Yes, the harbour, too, was ideal for yachtsmen—potentially. Actually, at that time, ten

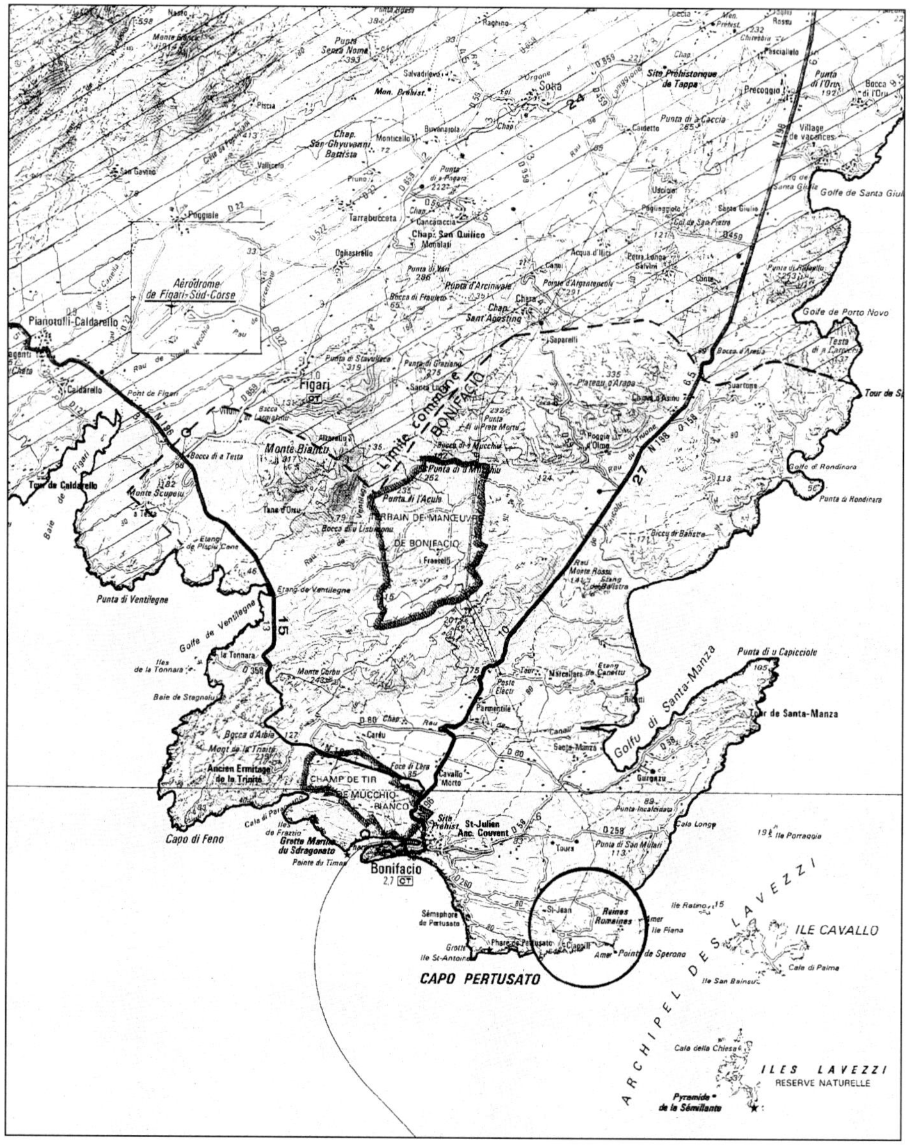

Map of the Bonifacio *canton*

Aerial view of Bonifacio,
taken in 1987

years ago, there were a number of snags. The French Navy had stopped using the spacious bottom end of the harbour; but this was still out of bounds to yachts. On the remaining stretch of harbour front there was little water, and the moorings were bad; yachtsmen found themselves in among the fischermen's boats, whose owners were not pleased. Yet the geographical location of Bonifacio was perfect for Mediterranean yachtsmen; and the setting of the sheltered harbour, dominated by a twelfth-century fortress, was superb.

Up to this point, Jacques and Guy had simply been looking for somewhere where they could occasionally get away from it all, and sail in peace. But now, standing on the Bonifacio harbour front, outside the disused French Navy barracks, they must—I suspect—have looked at one another with a wild surmise. To them, as yachtsmen, the challenging idea of transforming Bonifacio into an ideal yachting harbour proved to be irresistible. And, once they had decided to accept that challenge, one thing led to another—and then another.

For Bonifacio is the chief town of a large commune that embraces all those empty beaches and those stretches of uninhabited *maquis* which they had been admiring. If the Dewez Brothers were going to develop Bonifacio as a yachting centre, it would make sense also to develop the surrounding district as an international holiday region. For that purpose, two things would be essential: an easy way of getting to southern Corsica from Continental Europe—and sufficient water on the spot. . . .

What, in fact, was required was a coherent overall plan for the region as a whole. So the Dewez embarked on a general survey of the potentialities for a yachting harbour, some real estate development, a dam, and an airport. . . .

The Dewez brothers, themselves scions of a prosperous banking family, formed a private partnership with interested relations and friends; and, between them, they have invested 13 millions francs (about £1 million).

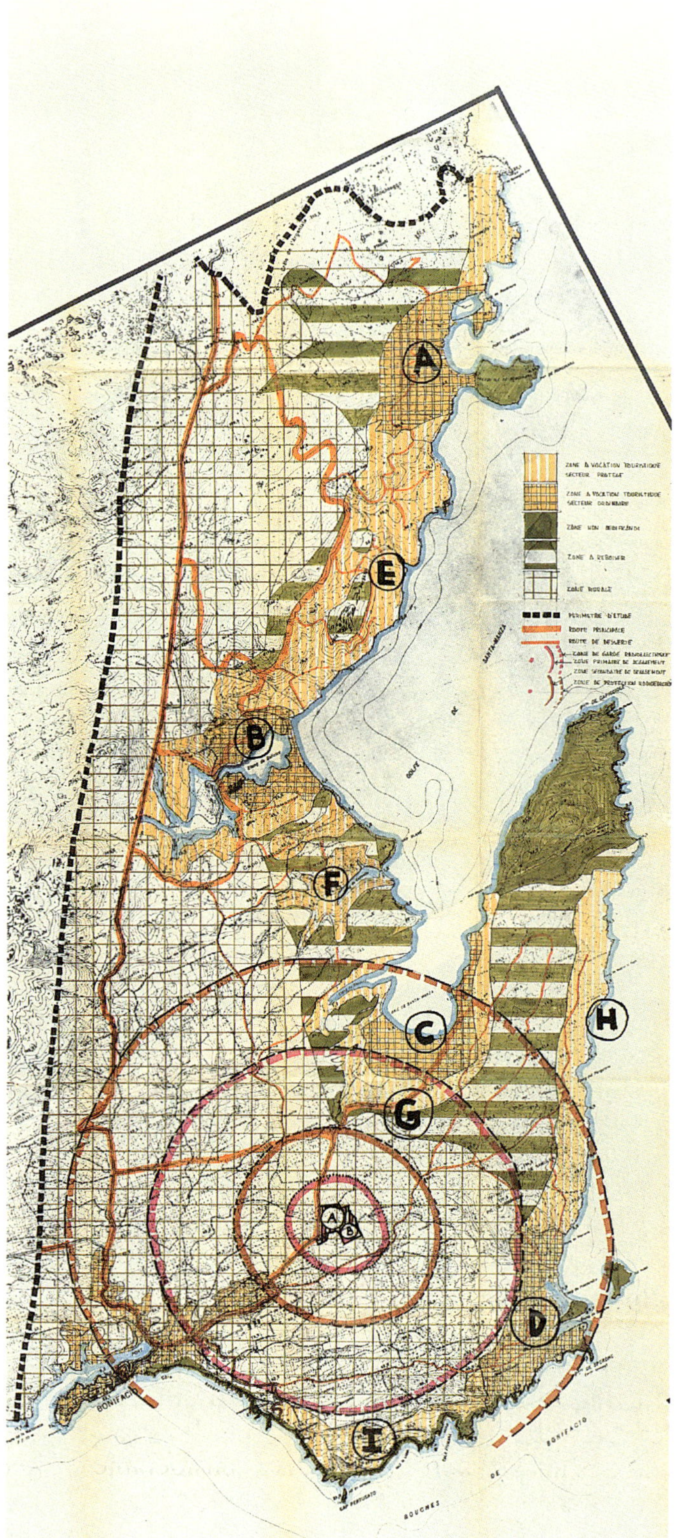

Development plan for Bonifacio *canton* (1965)

This Dewez group then set up a limited company, called CORSAREC (Société d'Aménagements Résidentiels et Récréatifs en Corse). Jacques, himself a former officer in the French Fleet Air Army, approached the Ministry of Armament, and obtained a 50-year lease on the Navy's sector of Bonifacio harbour. This included the old Naval barracks and officers'mess, which the Dewez proceeded to convert into a club house for their newly established Yachting Centre of Bonifacio. At the same time work began on the complete overhaul, renovation and extension of the harbour facilities.

The second priority project was to begin the conversion of some of those thousands of empty acres and miles of empty coast into a region where people who loved the sea could come, either to live permanently, or to spend their holidays on a variety of different "levels", from the popular lagoonside holiday village to the first-class hotel. So the Dewez group set up two property companies which bought those 30,000 acres at Sperone and Balistra, with a sea-coast eight miles long. The land was not expensive. What was going to be very costly was the installation of services—roads, water, electricity, telephones. These were destined to work out at 32,000 francs (or about £2,800) per acre.

If the scale of these operations conjures up the image of a pair of hard-faced, ruthless property tycoons, you can forget it. Because Jacques Dewez (pronounced, in French, Devez) and Guy Dewez (confusingly pronounced, in English, Due-ez) are preeminently gentle men.

Guy, more English than English, a former wartime anti-tank officer in the Royal Artillery, could easily be taken for an old-time English squire—clothes, courtesy, dogs, and all. I would guess that Jacques (the younger French brother, who is also bilingual) is more at home among the bright night lights of Paris than Guy. But, for both brothers, the sea's the thing. Jacques, besides his passion for yachts, is a considerable deep sea diver and explorer of shipwrecks and searcher for amphorae.

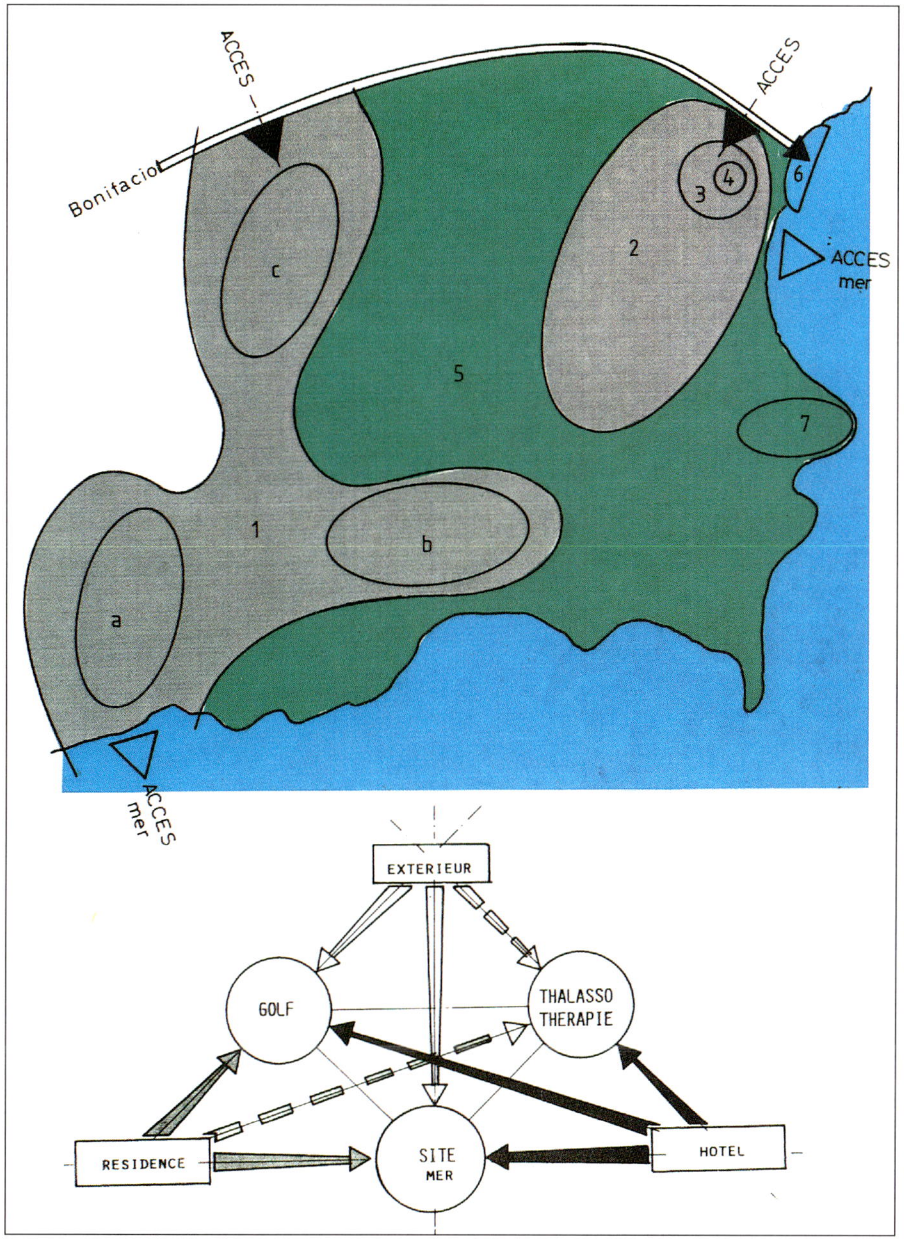

Site plan:
1: Residential lots (a. Ciappili, 35 acres; b. Hauts de Sperone, 32 acres; c. Falatte, 30 acres)
2: The Hameau and residential lots (30 acres)
3 and 4: Hotel, conference centre and thalassotherapy (7 acres).
5: Golf course, unconstructed area (193 acres)
6: Wharf
7: Archaeological excavations
The coverage per lot is 4 %

The Ciappili *mas* in 1963

Ciappili in 1974: early
stage of the development

Both brothers evoke evident warmth from the people who, in Paris and Corsica, work for them. Laurent, who runs the clubhouse in Bonifacio, was Jacques's *chef d'escale* in the days after the war when Jacques ran his private airline from Nice. Laurent, with his stupendous moustachios and corrugated face, looks like the archetypal Corsican bandit—despite the fact that he is native of Nice. In their Paris office the Dewez brothers share a bilingual secretary, who is Georges Carpentier's daughter.

To that office in the Boulevard Haussman Guy, who likes English cars and has just bought a Mini, walks every morning from his flat near the Etoile. (Neither brother is a chauffeur-driven-tycoon type: Jacques was, at one time, himself a successful racing driver.) It's a natural walk for someone who is as fascinated by architecture, ancient and modern, as is Guy.

It was because the brothers were keen to create a residential "village" of an architecturally unusual kind that one of the first steps they took in their Corsican development was to earmark for this purpose about 40 acres around the green valley of Ciappili, four miles east of Bonifacio. . . .

So they considered all kinds of houses—"We even looked at metal ones"—and consulted several architects. Finally, they decided upon the kind of material they felt would be right for the Ciappili setting: red Canadian cedar-wood, which needs hardly any maintenance, and resists the sea-air. . . . The French were shaken. What! Invest capital in a wooden house?!? For them, security is a house of stone: pierre—a word to conjure with. . . .

In the local press, doubts about the ultimate fate of the beaches have also been ventilated. . . . "Our policy for the beaches," says Guy Dewez, "is to open them up gradually, as we make arrangements for adequate access, parking facilities, maintenance and services. Otherwise, the beaches might immediately be turned into rubbish shoots. There are plenty like that, already."

Ciappili: development plan with a section of the valley

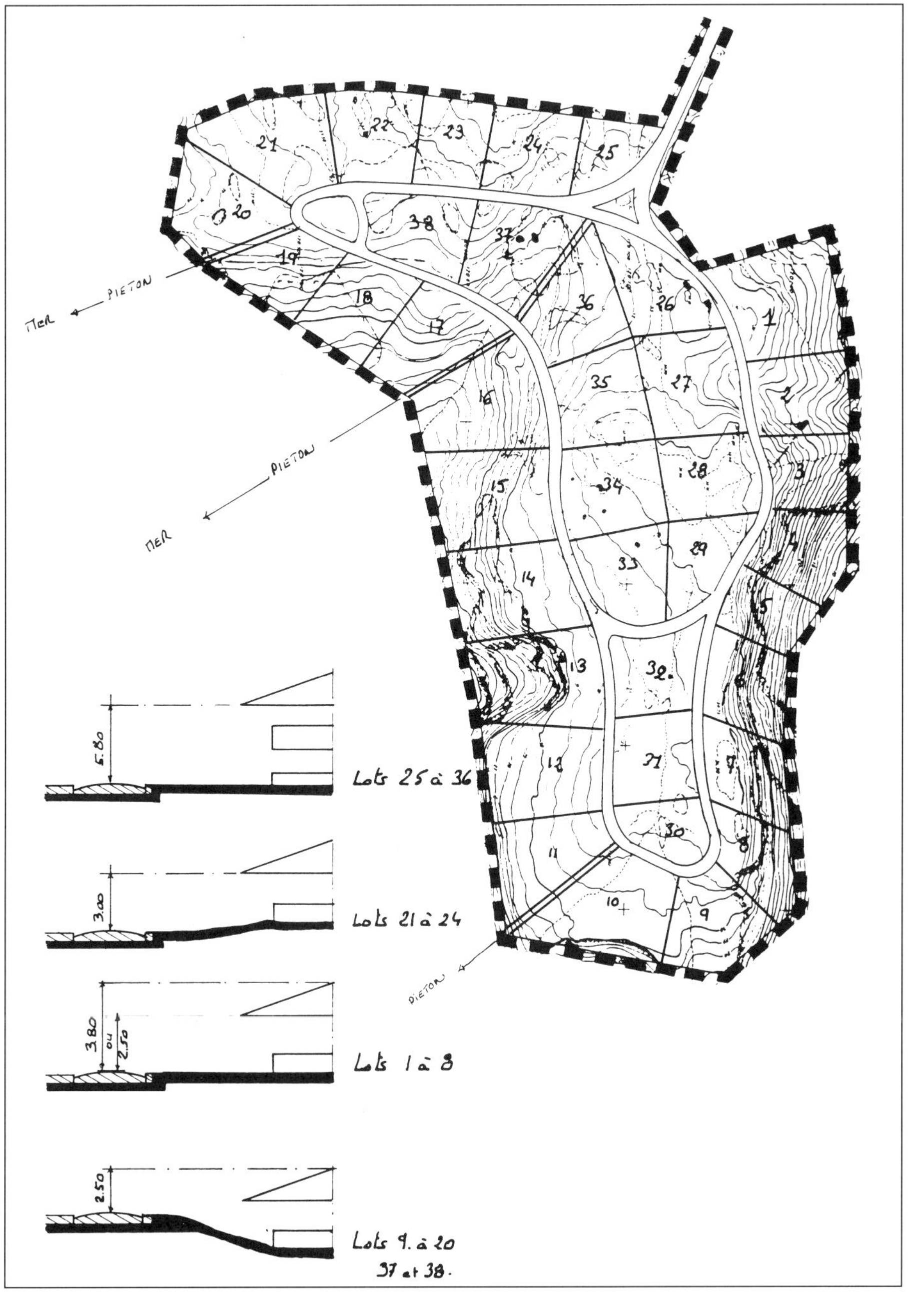

The Hauts de Sperone: development plan. The average lot is 27,000 square feet

My own clear impression is that Jacques and Guy Dewez, themselves escapees from the Côte d'Azur, really care about the seascape and the landscape, and about the people who live and work in it. . . .

The Dewez, after building and selling the first four cedar-wood houses, had decided to sell plots, not houses, in the future. This enables the people who buy the plots to build their own houses to one of three general designs, with personal modifications. . . .

The purchasers, says Jacques Dewez, "really select themselves". They are people who like the sea, and peace: not ones to hunger after nightclubs or other forms of riotous living. It is noticeable that the Dewez brothers have become personally friendly with practically all the people, of whatever nationality, who have bought property at Ciappili.

There are still difficulties in getting domestic help; and the shops are four miles away. Still, Xavier, the "caretaker" of the Ciappili "village", whose family sold the land to the Dewez group, has started a market-gardening project, which will supply Ciappili residents with some fruit and vegetables, as well as creating a modest number of jobs. Xavier is also responsible for a tree-planting programme, reforestation in and around Ciappili village.

On a wider, more ambitious scale, the Dewez brothers intend to try and resuscitate the region's agriculture: especially the cultivation of olives, which was once a flourishing way of life in these parts. Hopefully, too, they will try to give a fillip to the local fishing industry which, though it produces what are probably the best lobsters in the Mediterranean, has seldom been highly regarded in Bonifacio. . . .

Today, most of the townspeople seem happy enough, with the Dewez harbour development. This yields a handsome bonus in tourism, because, though Bonifacio is short of hotels and rooms, the yachtsmen come in and buy food in the shops, while living on their boats in the harbour. The restaurants have profited, too; and the Dewez brothers make a point of ringing the changes on the restaurants where they and their friends eat, in the hope of preventing jealousy. But the locals who care for such things do seem to be aware that, though boutiques have sprung up like mushrooms, the Dewez brothers are determined to play their part in preventing the district from becoming unbalanced by an unbridled escalation of tourism, of the kind that has rendered the Côte d'Azur insufferable.

"In fact," says Guy Dewez, "Bonifacio is not, and never can be, in the same category as St Tropez. Its development potential is based mainly on sea sports and, especially, racing by sail. It is true that the harbour installations will be largely used by cruising vessels, but Bonifacio will never be half as easily accessible by car as the Côte d'Azur resorts." And that in itself, Guy Dewez believes, will limit the numbers. . . .

The business of getting these developments off the ground has meant years of persistently hard work and exertion for the Dewez brothers, who seem never to take a real holiday. It also required an important outlay of capital, with no immediate return. When there are a sufficient number of boats using the harbour, and a sufficient number of plots have been sold at Ciappili, the big investments on installations and services for those two projects will have paid off. But, meanwhile, the other two of the original four Dewez group investments—those 30,000 acres of land at Sperone and Balistra—are increasing in value all the time.

At any moment it is open to the group to take the profit on part of their existing investments, and then reinvest—possibly with additional partners—in further developments. . . .

"What we aim to do," Guy Dewez told me, "is to establish a community whose members, while united by love of the sea, have a varied range of other interests as well. So the homes we build will be split into distinct groups for bachelors and families without children, families with teenagers, families with young children, old

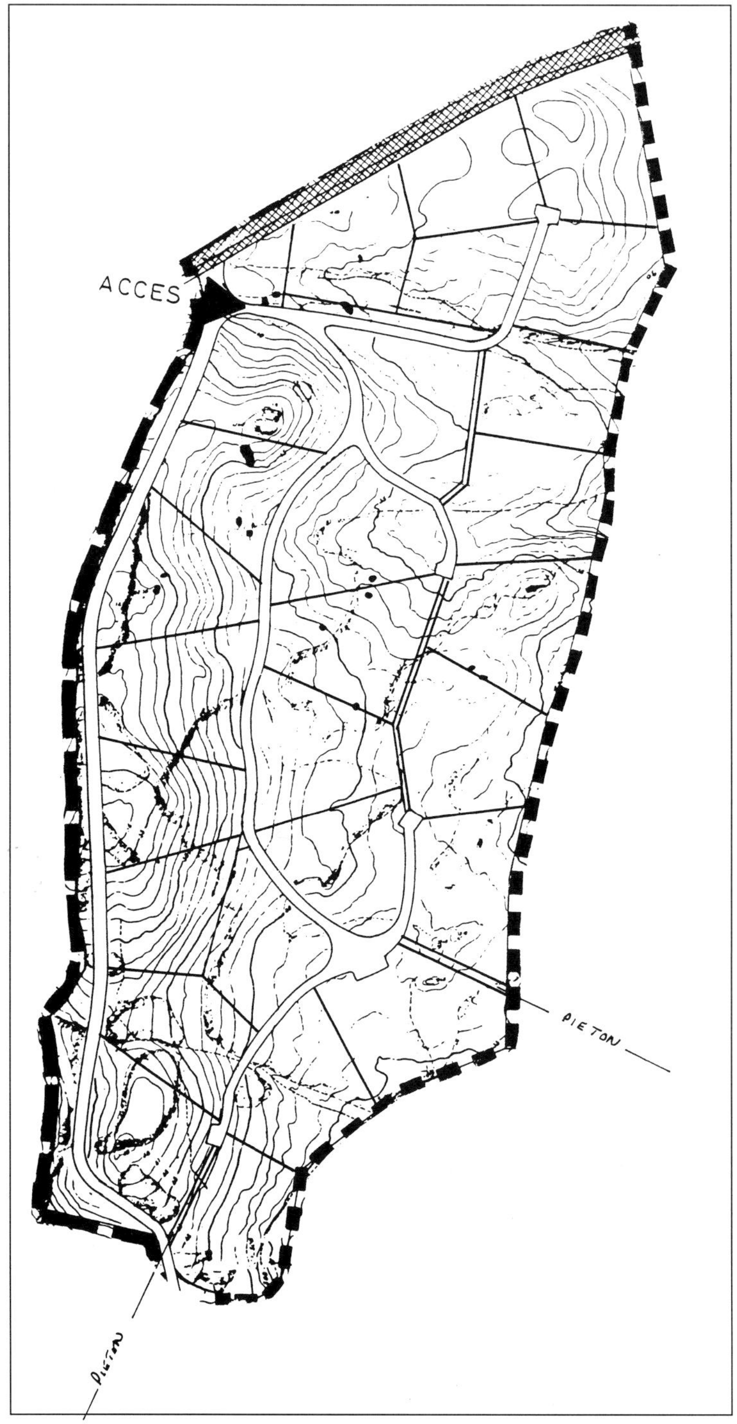

Falatte: development plan. The lots, an average of 48,000 square feet each, are staggered in relation to each other

people living together or alone. Each of these groups will have its own services—shops, restaurants and, according to the particular needs, crêches, youth clubs, and so on. . . .

At the same time, a 200-room hotel will be built by the Lagoon of Piantarella, with a sports centre for riding and tennis, and a medical centre close by. A place will be reserved, too, for the building of a cultural centre with theatre, exhibition hall, art gallery, library, photographic laboratory. . . .

"Finally, and most important," Guy Dewez added, with gentle emphasis, "a large part of the area will be left in its natural state."

LIONEL BIRCH

It may seem a little quixotic to devote thirty years to a single property development, especially in an age of increasing short-termism, and especially for a property of 325 acres, only 134 of which have been built on. But that is the time it has taken to develop the Sperone domain in Corsica. In the early sixties, pressure to develop the French coastline, particularly in the south, was intense. It was this that prompted Guy and Jacques Dewez to explore the island of Corsica (a French region in its own right, since divided into two *départements*).

Their search for a property as a long-term investment was also shaped by their love of sailing. They were drawn to the south of the island, to its remarkable landscape and coastline, and in particular to the southernmost city of Bonifacio and its immediate surroundings.

The commune of Bonifacio is the largest in Corsica and boasts 44 miles of shoreline. The town is striking. Its spacious, sheltered, deepwater harbour, then used primarily by local fishermen, was an ideal permanent mooring-place for keel boats and there was space to provide maintenance and chandlery services.

The Dewez brothers began to envision a project that would involve leasing and developing the navy's share of the harbour so as to attract yacht owners; buying two properties totalling more than 900 acres—one of which had a lagoon fed by a river with headwaters in the mountains (Corsica is very dry in summer); and building a small number of high-quality houses on the other.

They formed a private company and on 7 April 1962 bought the Sperone domain, a 325-acre property south-east of Bonifacio overlooking the 12-mile-wide straits that separate Corsica from Sardinia. In August of the following year, they bought the 570-acre Balistra domain where there was a potential site for a substantial reservoir. Both properties consisted of virtually untouched littoral.

Almost ten years went by before the first houses were built on the Sperone domain; it was essential to win the consensus of the local population before construction could begin. Guy and Jacques Dewez collaborated closely with the local authorities from the beginning and, before long, became increasingly involved with the strategy for the development of south-east Corsica as a whole, not just at the local level but also with the central government. The overriding concern was to avoid the mistakes that had been made on the southern coast of France.

Even so, before development of any kind at Bonifacio could be made worthwhile, the area had to become more accessible. The nearest airports with regular services to the French mainland were at Ajaccio and Bastia, more than 85 and 105 miles away, and the roads were poor. A month after buying the Sperone domain, Jacques Dewez—a former fighter pilot with the French navy—and his brother carried out an aerial reconnaissance flight and pinpointed the Figari valley, 12 miles from Bonifacio, as the only potential site for an international airport. After two years of study and of enlisting local support, they presented a proposal to the Corsican regional authority. It was accepted, only to be thrown out by the equivalent of the Civil Aviation Authority, which was more interested in developing an airport at Calvi. In the end, the plan for Figari prevailed. Work began in

1973 and twenty years later, the airport was already handling more than a quarter of a million passengers a year.

Although by constructing a dam at Balistra they thought they could provide enough water for anything then envisaged for the Sperone domain, they nevertheless commissioned a comprehensive hydrogeological study to survey the overall needs of people living in the town of Bonifacio. The conclusion was that if they built a reservoir with a capacity of over 1 billion gallons at Balistra, there would be ample water for everyone in the area for the foreseeable future. They presented their report in 1971. This happened to coincide with a decision by the Corsican authorities to make their own study of water provision in the south of the island. Two new reservoirs were built elsewhere, but the Balistra lagoon remains a valuable reserve.

By 1971, the only tangible evidence of nine years' effort was a yacht club and yachting centre on the harbour at Bonifacio (the former naval barracks and officers' mess), a chandlery, a boatyard and a marine engineering service. Since the entire project had been planned as an *investissement patrimonial*, which is to say an investment that makes its profits operationally, it was essential to begin the building project at the Sperone domain.

The first houses were built in the valley of Ciappili, a 40-acre site covered, like the rest of the estate, with an apparently robust but actually highly vulnerable *maquis*, with plants such as juniper, myrtle and ilex. Its fragility was one of the factors that governed the singular style of architecture that has come to characterize Sperone. As the *Architectural Review* commented twenty years later, "Timber is not a material often associated with French architecture," but that is what they chose.

There were various reasons for this decision. They wanted to interfere as little as possible with the terrain and plant life on a site that was physically challenging, with steep slopes and granite outcrops, and timber al-

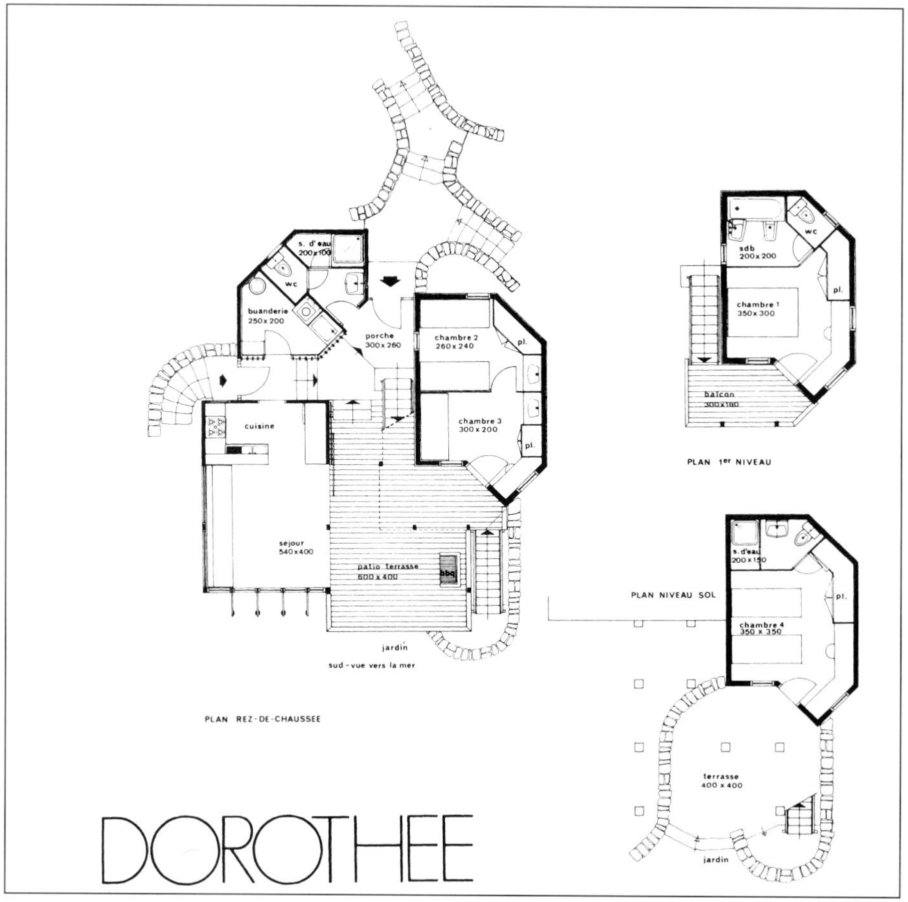

DOROTHEE

lowed for a more flexible response. Added to that, they were attracted both by the aesthetics of Charles Moore's Sea Ranch in Sonoma County, north of San Francisco, and by the recently completed French ski resort at Avoriaz, both built of red cedar. This timber requires minimal maintenance and weathers to a colour that harmonizes with the granite.

The four principals of the architectural group GEA (Groupement d'études architecturales)—Guy André, Guy Breton, Boguslaw Brzeczkowski and Jean-Marc Roques—had all worked on Avoriaz and some of them had studied in Berkeley, California, and were familiar with Sea Ranch. But at Ciappili this team of young architects began to create an architectural vernacular that developed in a very distinctive way over the next two decades.

Four houses were built. Then it was decided to sell plots with the proviso that the buyers build their own houses according to one of three general designs by GEA.

The project began well and attracted American and British owners as well as the French. But it was to be another ten years before the second phase of the development began, a decade marked by major local, regional and national political changes.

In the mid-seventies, a number of Pieds-Noirs (Algerian-born French who had left newly-independent Algeria ten years before) settled on the east coast of the island with the help of government grants. There was a violent demonstration by islanders during which two gendarmes were killed. The nationalist movement, until then an organization on the fringe of political life, stepped into the spotlight. For the next ten years there was intermittent bloodshed, attacks on foreign-owned property and economic disruption.

There were marked changes on the legitimate political stage too. During the presidency of Valéry Giscard d'Estaing (1974-1981), the central government embarked on a policy of decentralization. Planning permission was

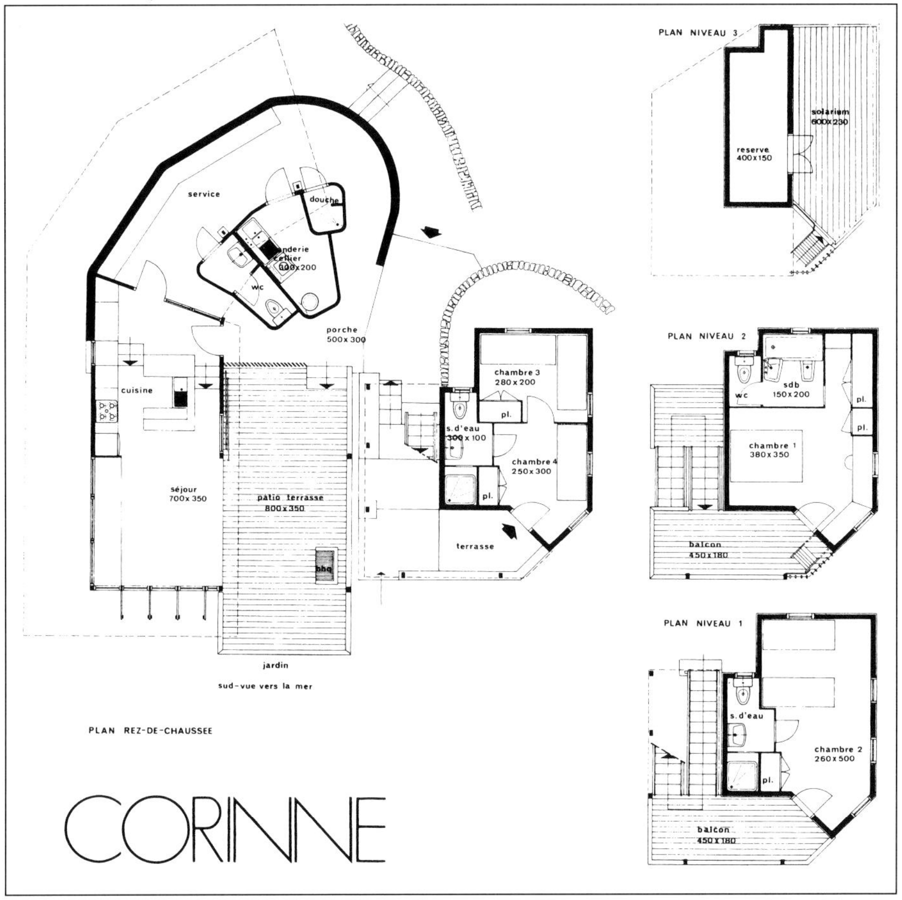

GEA Architects.
Floor plans of two houses designed in the early stage of the Ciappili development. These houses, like those that followed, are based on a helical plan; the rooms are thus laid out around a central deck

already in the hands of local mayors (who have party political allegiances as well as being representatives both of the state and the local community) together with the elected local council. Decentralization greatly increased their powers.

Environmental pressure groups then persuaded the government to introduce a "law of the littoral", an attempt to protect what remained of the French coastline from unbridled development. There was some resentment in Corsica, where local people felt they were already policing potential building projects vigorously. Commendable in its motivation, in practice the *loi du littoral* enabled those opposed to development of any kind, whether their objections were well-founded, cynical or simply frivolous, to delay proceedings by years. Nevertheless, a period of relative calm and growing prosperity in the early eighties enabled the Dewez brothers to begin the second phase of building at Ciappili. By 1985, demand had outstripped what was always going to be a limited supply.

They reconsidered their options, and after commissioning a study of the entire property from the architect and planner Pierre Puccinelli, they submitted an overall development scheme to the authorities, who granted planning permission a year later. The plan included plots at a site known as the Hauts de Sperone where there was space for large high-cost family houses intended for year-round use. The quality and imagination of GEA's work at Ciappili enabled the Dewez brothers to persuade the majority of clients to use the same architects and the same material: red cedar. So with one or two exceptions—notably by Jean Nouvel and Sir Norman Foster—the integrity of the original architectural philosophy was maintained while the architects were free to develop the ideas that had shaped Ciappili.

The first houses were constructed at the Hauts de Sperone in 1987, and two years later, work began at another site called Falatte. Altogether there were to be just over one hundred

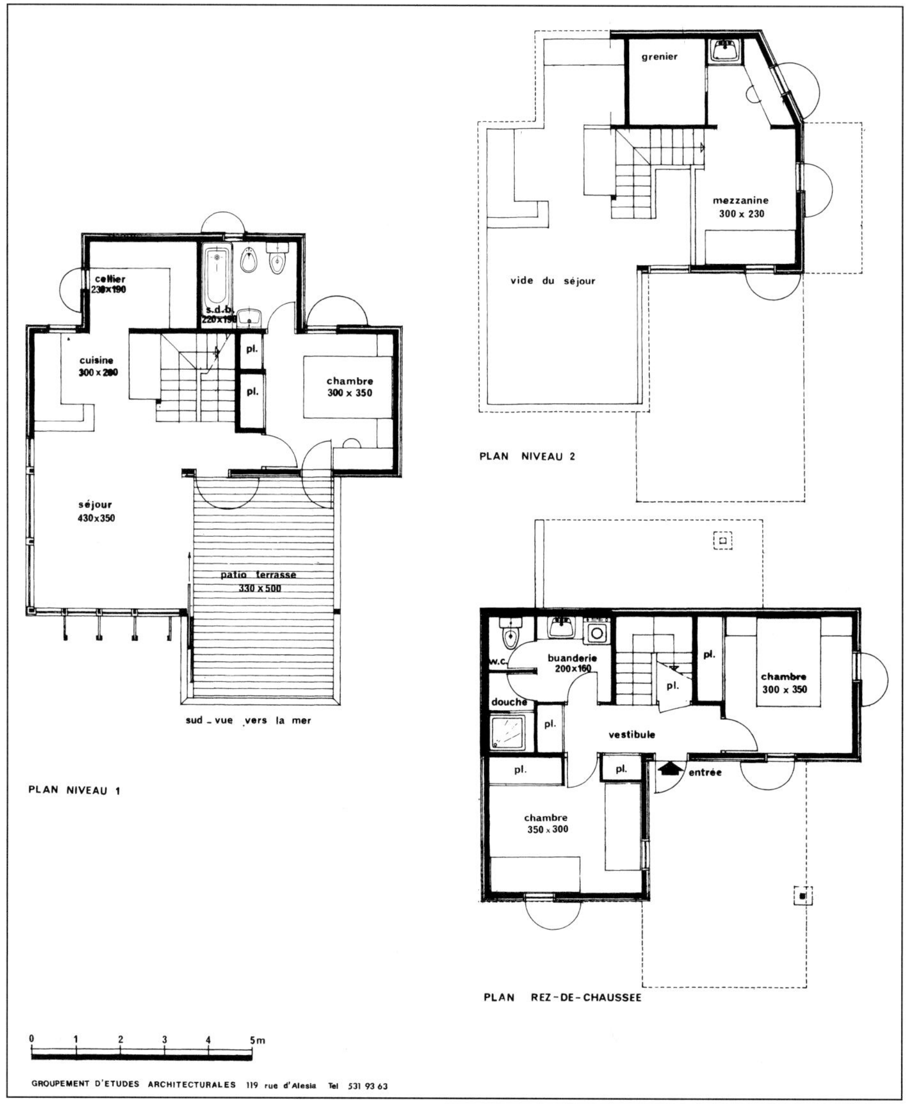

Alternative house plans in the beginning of the Ciappili development. Architects: GEA

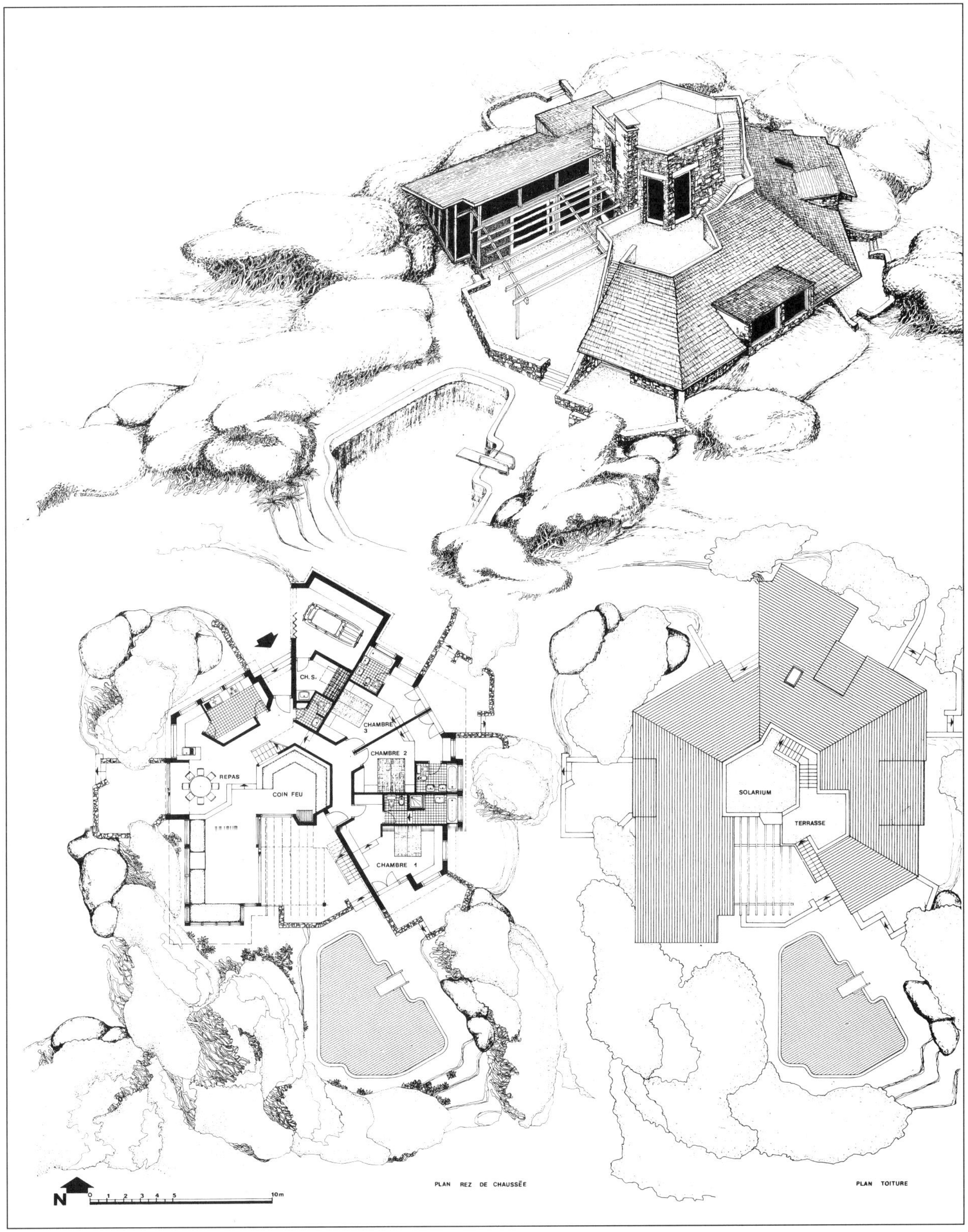
CH. S.
CHAMBRE 3
CHAMBRE 2
REPAS
COIN FEU
CHAMBRE 1
SOLARIUM
TERRASSE
N
0 1 2 3 4 5 10m
PLAN REZ DE CHAUSSÉE
PLAN TOITURE

houses, including those at Ciappili. The plan also included a 178-acre golf course, not least because on an island where hundreds if not thousands of acres of *maquis* go up in flames almost every summer, a golf course is an effective fire-break. The course was designed by the American Robert Trent Jones Sr., but apart from the greens, which were put in by specialists from outside the island, the rest of the work was carried out by Corsican contractors.

This has been a characteristic of the scheme as a whole. The initial idea was to bolster the local economy as much by employing local firms as by attracting people to the island to sail or to buy second homes. About ninety per cent of the building work, particularly the woodwork, was done by Corsican construction companies to immensely exacting standards.

The golf course was formally inaugurated in 1992 and in the same year, work began on the construction of a self-contained hilltop village called the Hameau de Piantarella, which was to include eleven villas and eighty apartments, the former designed by Pierre Puccinelli and the latter by Bruno Allais—the architect who was appointed construction supervisor of the whole development—Jacques Charrat and Philippe Vasseur. The architectural team was new but the architecture clearly drew on the work of GEA. Though the apartments were relatively small, from 645 to 1,400 square feet, and interconnected by walkways, the aim of the architects was to give each one the feel of an independent private house. They also strove to create structures that would have minimal impact on what was another piece of outstanding landscape.

The first twenty-six apartments had just been finished when a faction of the nationalist movement, which had been relatively passive during the last years of the French socialist administration, resumed an effensive against public and private targets. However, by the early nineties, the nationalist movement had undergone a fundamental change. The majority of active members had put down their weapons and their representatives were continuing the campaign by legitimate political means.

The other important difference was that, this time, the majority of Corsicans decided they had had enough of violence. It took courage for a population of only 200,000—most of whom must know, or know of, someone in the nationalist movement—to start to break the entrenched code of silence, but this is what began to happen. In 1994, the first public demonstrations against the violence took place and in an act of even greater significance, the island's women took to the streets in silent protest in early 1995.

But the campaign of violence was sufficiently dramatic to damage the confidence of potential buyers, to delay the completion of the village at Piantarella and to prevent, temporarily, the construction of a one-hundred-bed hotel and thalassotherapy centre which will complete the Sperone domain and attract visitors throughout the year.

Despite its low density, the high quality of the development makes it by far the largest in Corsica in terms of its budget. Some 150 million francs have already been spent, eighty per cent of which has gone to Corsican firms. And by the time the Hameau de Piantarella has been completed and the hotel commissioned, another 250 million francs will have been spent. In addition, close to 7.5 million francs have already gone into local taxes, and the amount increases by between 1.7 and 1.9 million annually. The project has created between thirty and forty permanent jobs, and attracted a clientele of hundreds, all of whom contribute to the economy by using local shops and restaurants.

As to the architecture of the Sperone domain and its place in this very special landscape, the photographs that follow speak for themselves.

CIAPPILI

Two views of Ciappili

Ciappili was the first area of the domain to be developed, and seeing the valley today, nearly twenty years after building began, the success of the architectural texture is the most remarkable feature. In the photographs published in *The Daily Telegraph* in 1973, the raw newness of the wood of the houses is quite striking, and it is hard to imagine that the process of mellowing and blending would have been so rapid. This is a vindication of the long-term vision of the Dewez brothers and their architects. The surrounding vegetation has also grown in profusion, increasing the impression that the houses are natural growths, rather than man-made elements.

At the same time, the houses have taken on a second patina of time through the personalities of their owners. One of the earliest houses, placed high up on the ridge, always boasts a bright hand-painted banner flying from the top roof-ridge—the subtle and warm colours of the flag are found in the owners' own paintings and watercolours that fill the house. Others, like the Ferreri house in the first chapter, or the Pochy house described here, have bright notes of colour in their gardens, which flicker into view like landmarks for someone traveling around the area. The same vocabulary of architectural forms, mediated by different owners, gives some houses an air of quiet contemplation, others a quiver of welcome and activity, even when the houses are empty.

Many of the present owners first visited the site without any intention of settling there, but the valley and the sea worked their charm. Jacques Dewez points out that at Ciappili, as at Sperone and Falatte later, the setting was its own salesman! The pace of life at Ciappili has a Mediterranean languor to it, compounded by the scent of wild rosemary and thyme from the pervading *maquis*. It does not have the artificial bonhomie of a holiday village—indeed, several of the houses are inhabited all year round; it has, instead, a gentle sense of well being.

THE OWNER'S DESCRIPTION

Just about ten years ago, the dashing *Rose de Jericho*, in full sail and driven by a light south-easterly wind, discovered the sloping, perfectly aligned dark wood roofs of a few homes nestled in the valley of Ciappili. The elegant black ketch, curious as always, drew closer, moving from rock to rock, and finally cast anchor near the beach.

The crew set foot on the ground without the slightest idea of building a house there, because they knew their boat would never accept it. Yet the scent of the *maquis*, the golden yellow of the mimosas, and the light and shadows filtering through the pine trees enchanted the explorers.

Wouldn't a "lookout point" perched at the top of a house be the ideal spot to observe the sea, the boats and the changing colours of the Lavezzi granite?

Furthermore, chains, sails, cranks and other nautical equipment could be stored in a mezzanine. And a kitchen corner, a small living room with a wood stove, a guest bedroom, and a dormitory for the shipmates on the ground floor could all live in harmony with nature.

This fleeting image became a reality one chilly autumn when the *Rose de Jericho* preferred the soft winds and protected anchorages along the miles of southern Corsican coastline.

While the *Rose* frolicked, the crew on shore embraced the bluish black colours and kept company with Jean-Marc, Guy, Italo and Lucien. When the final nail was driven, they saw – from the top of the "scaffolding" – that other strange wooden constructions were going up. They saw the magical transformation of the *maquis* into a large green garden where men followed around little white balls. They also met a great many good friends. Finally, the crew constructed a false-real painting studio and two new rooms (for other friends of the sea).

Today, the crew hopes that all this does not make the beautiful black ketch jealous, now that it is back in the heavenly waters of the Straits of Bonifacio.

YVES POCHY

THE POCHY HOUSE
ARCHITECTS: YVES POCHY AND GEA

At Ciappili there are few formal hedges or marked boundaries. The access roads are marked by white stones, and occasional flights of stone steps run from the roads to houses at levels above and below. Indeed, if you are unfamiliar with the estate, it can sometimes be difficult to find the path to a particular house, even when you have it in view. At Ciappili, unlike Sperone, most of the houses are not directly accessible from the roadways—you often have to walk through the *maquis*. This creates an air of quiet magic and, occasionally, surprise. One such surprise is the Pochy house.

To reach it, you walk through the screen of bushes and low trees, to be met by an intriguing sight, the trunk of a dead tree, still standing but with branches lopped, and painted a deep Klein blue that pales to cerulean at the top. The tree flanks a wide, stepped deck that runs down to a small fountain and ornamental pool on one side, and back into the frame of the house itself on the other. But as you step into the ring of grey-green *maquis*, it is the tree that catches the eye.

Guy Dewez once called Marion and Yves Pochy's house *"la vigie"*—the lookout point. This seems an odd title for a house so centred on its own strange garden, but then you see the stairway rising to the top level, well above the vegetation, where an open deck over the main bedroom offers a magnificent view over the sea. The different levels of the house are not merely separated by elevation, but by their relationship to the wider world, one enclosed within the grass and *maquis*, the other open to the sea.

The lookout deck sits on a gantry over the main living area, an open-fronted double-height cube, which serves as meeting and eating place and artist's studio, with an enclosed living room to one side and kitchen to the other. At first this makes the house seem like an exploded

The Pochy house terrace

Main façade

diagram, and the mind's eye fills in the "missing" walls. The mannered gesture of the painted tree (a lilac that, when mature, reached to the height of the first floor; another one has been planted to replace it) seems less so once the surprising design of the house is appreciated.

The design of the living area might seem somewhat theatrical—it has, in fact, been used as a set for a performance. This was *La Nuit des Cadenas*, a short piece written by Bernard Kouchner and performed by other residents of Ciappili. Future historians of drama will no doubt aptly compare it with Pope's *The Rape of the Lock*, for its mock-heroic treatment of a mundane subject. The play, written in alexandrines, supposedly dealt with the problem of reserving

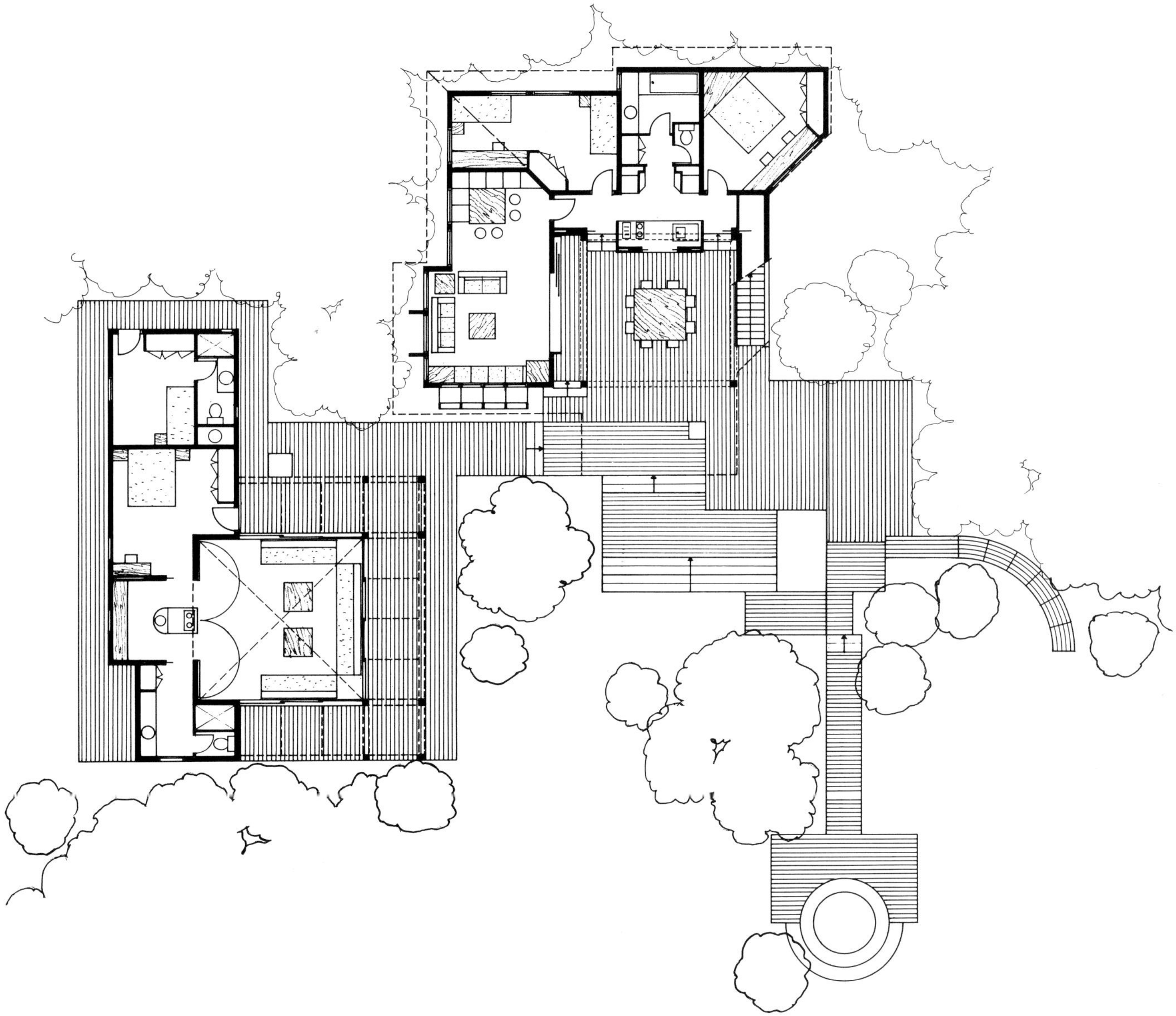

Ground floor of the Pochy house and annex. Architects: Yves Pochy and GEA

Two views of the open-air living room with the master bedroom (opposite)

times on the tennis courts, and most of the notable figures of Sperone figured among the dramatis personae. Guy Dewez, for example, was portrayed as a Renaissance cardinal, reflecting his interest in Italian architecture, and Jacques Dewez, who had recently sailed across the Atlantic single-handedly, as an admiral. Christine Ockrent performed the role of Chorus from the impromptu television screen of the serving hatch.

Yves Pochy is an architect and interior designer, and his wife an accomplished painter. Their house is both a personal and a professional statement, even though the owners describe the living area as a false-real one. They first came to Ciappili while cruising in their yacht, and had little interest in locking themselves onto the shore. But like so many others, they were entranced by the area, by the garden of houses growing out of the hillsides, by the views of the sea and the granite islands of the Lavezzi archipelago, and by new and old friends sharing their new life. In tribute to the ketch that first brought them there, and which is now moored in the harbour at Bonifacio, they planned their house (with Jean-Marc Roques), like a ship, with galley, quarters for the deck hands, deck and sail-loft, and, of course, the lookout point.

Beside the house is a new addition, which is something between a summer house and a guest wing. The fact that it comprises only a single, low storey emphasizes the open arch of the main living area. The floor plan of the new building is square, and the glass walls on three sides are shaded from the sun by wooden lattice roofs over the walkways. Inside, the space is divided by a folding interior wall that opens to reveal a cooking area, bathroom and bedroom/study. The low ceiling and precise proportions of the main room recall Japanese interiors, an effect heightened by the simple floor cushions and low tables with which the room is furnished. The walls and floor are in polished wood, and the wood finish outside

The annex (above) and an overall view of the house

matches that of the main house. The whole is sited carefully to integrate with the main house, but its individual design creates a different ambience, adding to the richness of the multi-layered whole.

Interior of the Japanese-style room in the annex

THE IKAM HOUSE
ARCHITECTS: GEA

James Elroy Fleeker, the least bad of the English late Romantic poets, has a line about seeing "old ships like swans asleep, beyond the village that men once called Tyre". This calm and elegiac verse came to mind the first time I saw the Ikam house, and in many ways this house, one of the latest to be built at Ciappili, represents the mature phase of this development.

The house was designed originally for Jacques Séguéla, and the present owners took it over when the former decided to build a new house on the Hauts de Sperone. Set into the slope of the valley at Ciappili overlooking the inlet to the sea, the house has now become part of the landscape, rather than an imposition on it. The wood has been allowed to weather until it has taken on the natural silver-grey tones of the *maquis*, and the surrounding vegetation has grown up, blurring the original outlines of the building.

In this form, the Ikam house echoes Bruno Allais' comments about the different styles for the developments on the domain. "A residential development such as we have created passes through several phases," he says. "There is the pioneering phase, when only a few plots have been built on, and everyone is caught up in a spirit of involvement. New arrivals are welcomed, the plans for their houses eagerly studied, ideas shared and compared. This grows into what I call the consolidation phase, when most of the plots have been built on or are being built on. This creates a real synergy between the different parties. It's a happy and enthusiastic time, and all sorts of initiatives, social and communal, arise. It's in this phase that the true sense of community takes root. And as the last plots are sold and built on, so the consolidation phase turns into an established phase. The social energy liberated earlier is channelled into

The Ikam house, half-hidden in its valley

Pine trees at the entrance
to the house

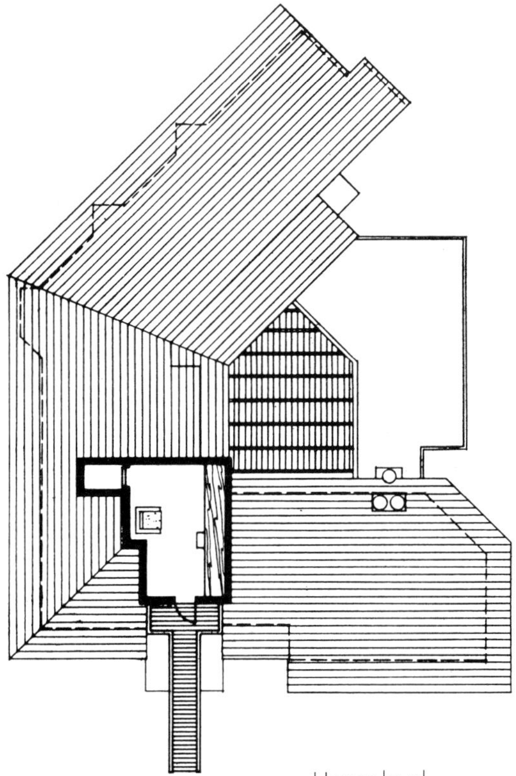

Upper level

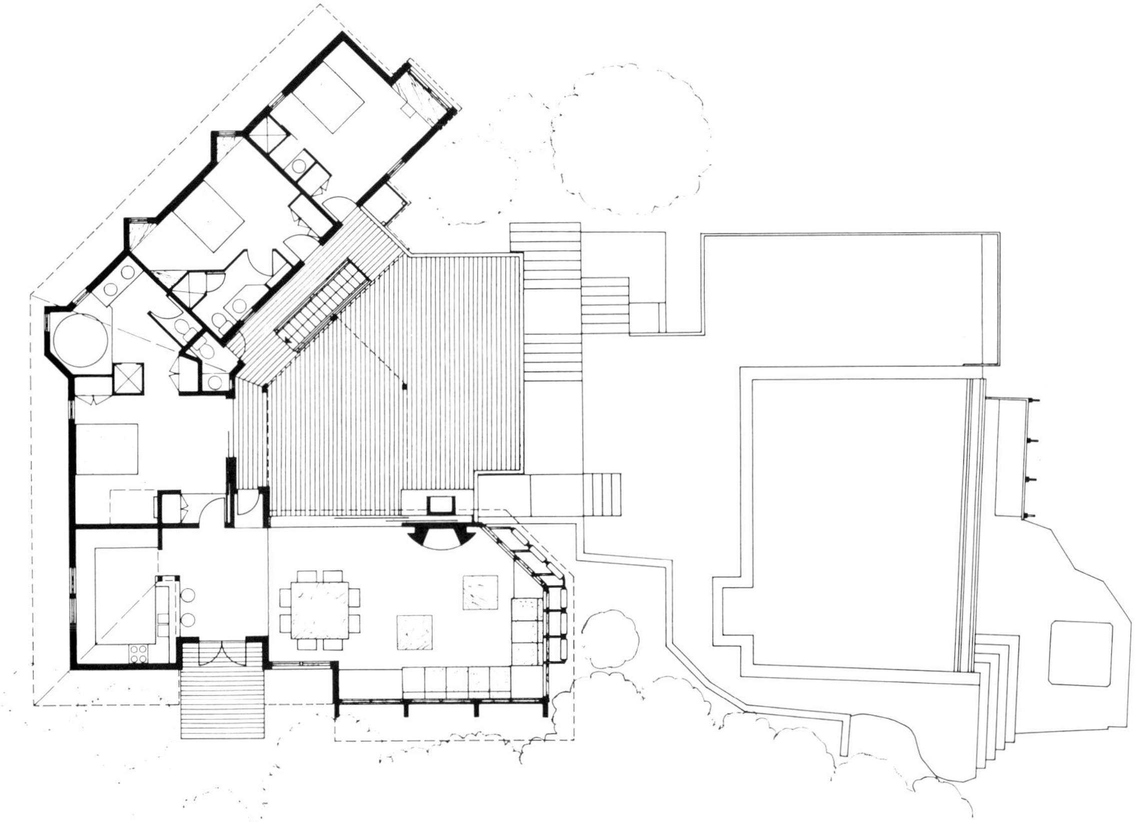

Plans for the upper levels of the Ikam house.
Architects: GEA

The Ikam house and the pool

firmer patterns of friendships, and as such, the community, having reached naturally its optimum state, stabilizes. So new developments become slightly less welcome, and changes to the pattern are looked on with more conservative eyes. This wholly human process of maturing is something the architects and managers of a development like ours need to keep in mind. On the Sperone domain each of the different areas is working at a different point in the cycle. Add to that the fact that each development has in turn provided a point of departure for the next—Ciappili for the Hauts de Sperone, the Hauts for Falatte, Falatte for Piantarella—and the social mix becomes a fascinating challenge.

"Imagine that an owner decides to paint his house white on the outside. Leaving aside the question of covenants and agreements, such a proposal would probably be met with concern and disquiet at Ciappili, be the subject of some debate on the Hauts, and be taken as an interesting novelty at Falatte! This isn't to say that the owners in one area or another differ radically in their attitudes, of course not. Most owners are very proud of their homes and happy with the community they share. Rather, the cyclical process I have mentioned has an invisible effect on us all."

The Ikam house itself visually sums up this established mode of quiet order at Ciappili. It seems to rise naturally from the landscape and be at one with it. The large wooden deck on the main floor vibrates gently underfoot, echoing the movement of trees and wind. The interiors have a careless, relaxed feel. Objects and furniture, it seems, are placed where they need to be, where they always have been. The house has a lived-in feeling, even when empty.

The floor plan of the building is a fan shape, with the rooms on the two main floors radiating out from the centre of the main deck. The bedrooms are on the lowest level (it makes little sense to speak of a "ground floor" on the slopes of Ciappili!), as is the pool. They overlook the

The terrace extending from the living room

Living room of the Ikam
house (above) and master
bedroom (opposite)

pool towards the sea, with smaller windows facing the *maquis*. On the main floor, the dining area and kitchen back directly against the rock of the valley side, increasing the sense of involvement with the landscape. At the top of the house, on the third level, is an open platform with views over the sea and the rest of the valley. Thus the house is both linked to the ground level and to the open sky. Guy Dewez describes this kind of layout as helical, as it traces an imaginary line that rises, corkscrew-like, through the layers and exterior edges of the house. The original house designs suggested in the Ciappili development followed such a layout, which exploits both the unusual and varied contours of the site, and the advantages and flexibility of wooden construction. The Ikam house can be seen as the most mature in this approach, and it is a vindication of the variety and value of the design.

THE HAUTS DE SPERONE

The Hauts de Sperone:
view of the lake

The development at the Hauts de Sperone began, as we have seen, some twenty years after the first houses at Ciappili were designed. During that period, the public appreciation of architecture improved, and there was a great deal of residential coastal development, of varying levels of quality, all around the Mediterranean. The clients attracted to the development at Sperone therefore arrived with approaches that differed from those of the pioneers at Ciappili. As the texts some people have provided about their homes show, they were all equally taken with the *esprit des lieux*, the sheer beauty of the sea and the unspoilt landscape. And in some cases, they wanted to make a more personal architectural statement. This appears in the slightly greater variety of architectural styles on the Hauts de Sperone, and in a different dialogue between architects and patrons. This dialogue is just as committed and as passionate as in the earlier work, but develops the earlier vocabulary further. The new clients offered GEA the chance to expand the skills they had mastered at Ciappili. This balance between continuity and innovation adds a special excitement to the houses on the Hauts de Sperone.

The houses are built on a promontory running south-eastward from Ciappili. On one side, the houses face directly out to sea, and on the return slope, they overlook the golf course, with the sea to the south. The seaward slope is less abrupt than the landward one, where the houses, such as the Bériot and Michel houses discussed in this chapter, are perched on what is virtually a cliff. As the size of the plots in the Hauts de Sperone are slightly larger than at Ciappili, where one side of the valley was deliberately kept free of buildings, many of the houses are also larger. This factor has also allowed individual owners a wide range of ways of expressing the character of their homes. It is surprising to realize that the Luc, Roux, and Feldman houses discussed here are virtually on adjacent plots. They each display a wholly individual style, yet by sharing a common building style, their harmony, as at Ciappili, is exquisite.

THE LUC HOUSE
ARCHITECTS: GEA

Along the roads of the domain, the profiles of houses rise from the surrounding landscape. Built of wood, tinted in pale greys or left to weather naturally, they often present a plain planked facade to the roadside, with wooden roof tiles that have blended under sun and wind into the natural colours of the landscape. One such house is the Luc house.

From the architect's plans, the Luc house resembles nothing so much as the bridge of an ocean-going ship. Laterally symmetrical, it has a central living area facing an open deck, with main and guest bedrooms in wings to either side. Alongside the main living area, and opening off it, is the kitchen. The rooms are all on

The Luc house and surrounding landscape

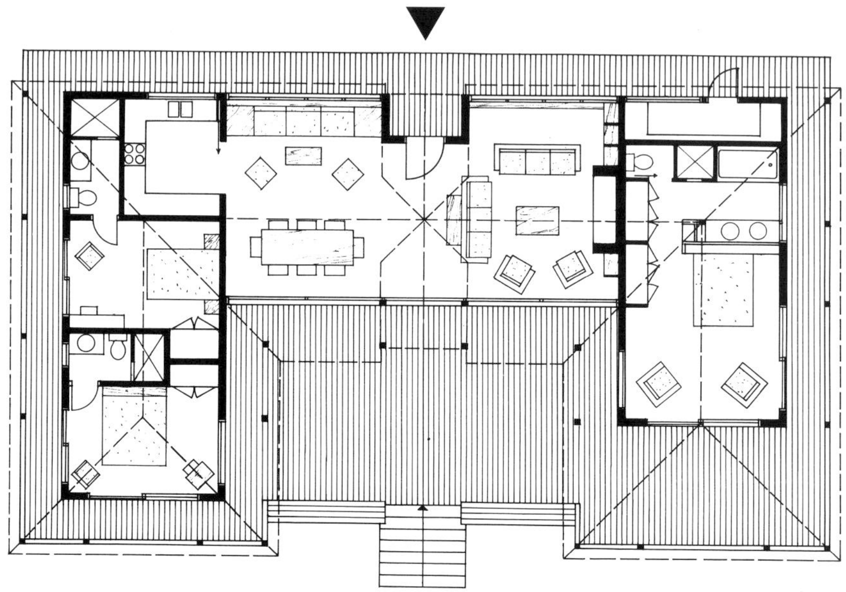

Plan of the Luc house. Architects: GEA

View of the house from the garden

The main deck. In the background, one of the guest bedrooms

one level, which occupies a total area of 807 square feet. The whole house faces decidedly out to sea. On the floor plan, the nautical virtues of practicality and simplicity can be seen in the arrangement of fitted seating, built-in bathrooms and well-defined kitchen area.

A different influence is reflected in the simple decorative details, such as the verandah in front of the living room, which provides a continuous shaded overhang for all the rooms. The idea of a house set within its own shade is Caribbean rather than Mediterranean; this influence is also visible in the slim white wooden pillars that support the roof. These are bisected by a plain white balustrade, which in turn is underpinned by white diagonal struts. This simple but effective composition is reminiscent of plantation houses in the West Indies, or the stark classical architecture of Louisiana.

Another classical detail appears in the roofline. The low pitch of the roof is cross-cut by a triangular pediment along the centre axis,

Beam structure in the living room

The living room

ending on the landward side in a window over the entrance door; on the seaward, in a window over the main deck. By providing visual interest to the roofline and linking the two facades through a common feature, this element holds the design together.

In the living room, the triangular opening which crosses the long axis of the room at its centre also provides an internal visual feature, in the roof beam structure itself. The windows in the pediment at either end allow light to enter from both sides; this passage of light is supplemented by narrow horizontal windows on the bays on either side of the entrance on the landward side. Standing in the living room, one can look out in both directions, inland towards the *maquis*, or out across the deck and garden to sea. This double lighting maximizes natural light throughout the day—indeed, many houses at Sperone enjoy a similar crossflow of light. It also creates a sense of location. Seen from the sea, the Luc house rises clearly from the landscape; within, its subtleties appear more distinctly.

The Luc house is one of the smaller houses on the Hauts de Sperone. It is on one level, with an axially symmetrical linear plan. Other larger houses, as will be seen, have several levels and more complex plans, yet use the same design and construction vocabulary. The success of the Luc house relies on detail: the proportions of the ceiling height to the floor plan, the way the overhanging verandah reaches across enough of the deck to lock the flanking rooms into the whole, the complex roof design created by the central light passage, and the use of lattice struts in the balustrade to evoke memories of another hemisphere.

Understatement leads to an understanding of this simple but satisfying house. Understatement is also part of the key to understading the Sperone domain as a whole. Simple materials handled with great craftsmanship, exacting planning and execution of details, and consummate skill in placing houses in the landscape—these lie at the heart of Sperone.

The master bedroom

THE OWNER'S DESCRIPTION

Like everyone else, I fell in love with the countryside the first day I saw it. I was also very impressed to see here the same architecture that I had just seen at Sea Ranch, in California. My wife, Sophie, and I constructed a first house at Ciappili; the friends we invited there were also taken in by the charm of the site.

When the Dewez brothers decided to construct on the Hauts de Sperone, we decided to build again. This time I wanted to bring some contemporary architecture to the area. The decision to use another architect, Jean-François Bodin, for our house encouraged other people to contact such great architects as Sir Norman Foster and our friend Jean Nouvel, for example.

Our concern was to create a house that was a reflection of its time, but that also created the groundwork for the future—which is necessarily linked to the past. The main themes of the house are space and transparency. The first large house at Sperone opened up the space and combined the Latin approach to volume with the equally Latin passion for materials. In the interior, for example, Sophie decided to use teak for the furniture she designed, which was manufactured in Indonesia. For the outside, I wanted to use the extraordinary qualities of the Corsican earth to create a garden that would reconcile the *maquis* and the house.

The first requirement of a vacation home is imagination, followed by comfort. We did everything possible to make sure that this space reflects and promotes the harmony of our couple and our creativity. The transparency of our house, for example, means that it moves and changes with the weather and the seasons. We created a home for all seasons to be able to use it in winter as much as in summer. It's very important to see a house, a site, in all seasons, as I am convinced that we are influenced by places and sites—it is not we who create a place; it is the place that creates us.

JACQUES and SOPHIE SÉGUÉLA

THE SÉGUÉLA HOUSE
ARCHITECT: J.-F. BODIN

The Séguéla house, designed by the architect Jean-François Bodin, was completed in 1992. It looks radically different from the other houses on the Hauts de Sperone—it is an interloper, even, with its glass and concrete frame. But, as we have seen, it is not Jacques and Sophie Séguéla's first home at Sperone—they built their first house at Ciappili in 1985, and, charmed by the area, introduced many of their friends to the development. And indeed, behind the novel appearance of the building lies a clear understanding of what can be called the "Sperone approach".

The house sits below the outer flank of the Hauts de Sperone, facing the fourteenth fairway to the sea. The hillside here is quite steep; the

The Sperone beach and the Séguéla, the Roux and the Feldman houses

Entrance walkway and interior views of house: the game room and the living room

house is reached from the parking area near the road via a walkway that enters the house at the first-floor level. From the walkway the general plan of the house is clear. The slightly pitched roof is divided into three main sections with intervening bands of skylights: the two end sections cover the bedroom areas, and the central roof covers the main living space between them. On the landward side, the house has a full glass curtain wall running two storeys high, with a similar wall on the first floor across the living area. On the seaward side, the living area projects out onto a deck, while the kitchen area runs back under the entrance walkway. The bedroom areas, which stand independently of the rear glass wall, have exterior wood panelling on the seaward side.

The central part of the living area rises to the roof, so that the visitor arrives at the first-floor level with a clear view down into it. Stairs at each end link the entrance with the living area and the bedroom units at the first-floor level. The seaward living area opens onto the

main space through unglazed window openings and a wide doorway, but the integrity of the bedroom sections is maintained by a physically independent structure, as well as by an elegant system of double doors. The bedroom units are painted on the outside in dark grey, but the walls facing into the living area are painted off-white, like the rest of the house (white wood panelling has also been used on the ground floor level). The separation between the various areas behind the glass curtain wall creates a series of different perspectives and spaces within the building, which emphasize its accessibility and openness.

While the design is symmetrical along the entrance axis, the carefully selected site adds variety. The northern bedroom unit looks out over steep *maquis* to the sea, while the southern unit looks out over a small enclosed garden. The bedrooms have shutters and windows that retract completely into the side walls, and these are aligned with the sets of entrance doors

The bedrooms open onto the glass wall. The windows and shades retract into the walls (opposite)

so that there is a view from the back of the house straight through to the sea beyond it. Jacques and Sophie Séguéla are particularly pleased with this feature. "Because we knew Sperone well, we knew that what we wanted was a house that would give a variety of views. Some people choose the single wide panorama: we like a range of choice that varies from room to room and from level to level."

Detail of the glass facade
and air view of the house

View of the garden: the
vertical sunscreens slide
along the walls

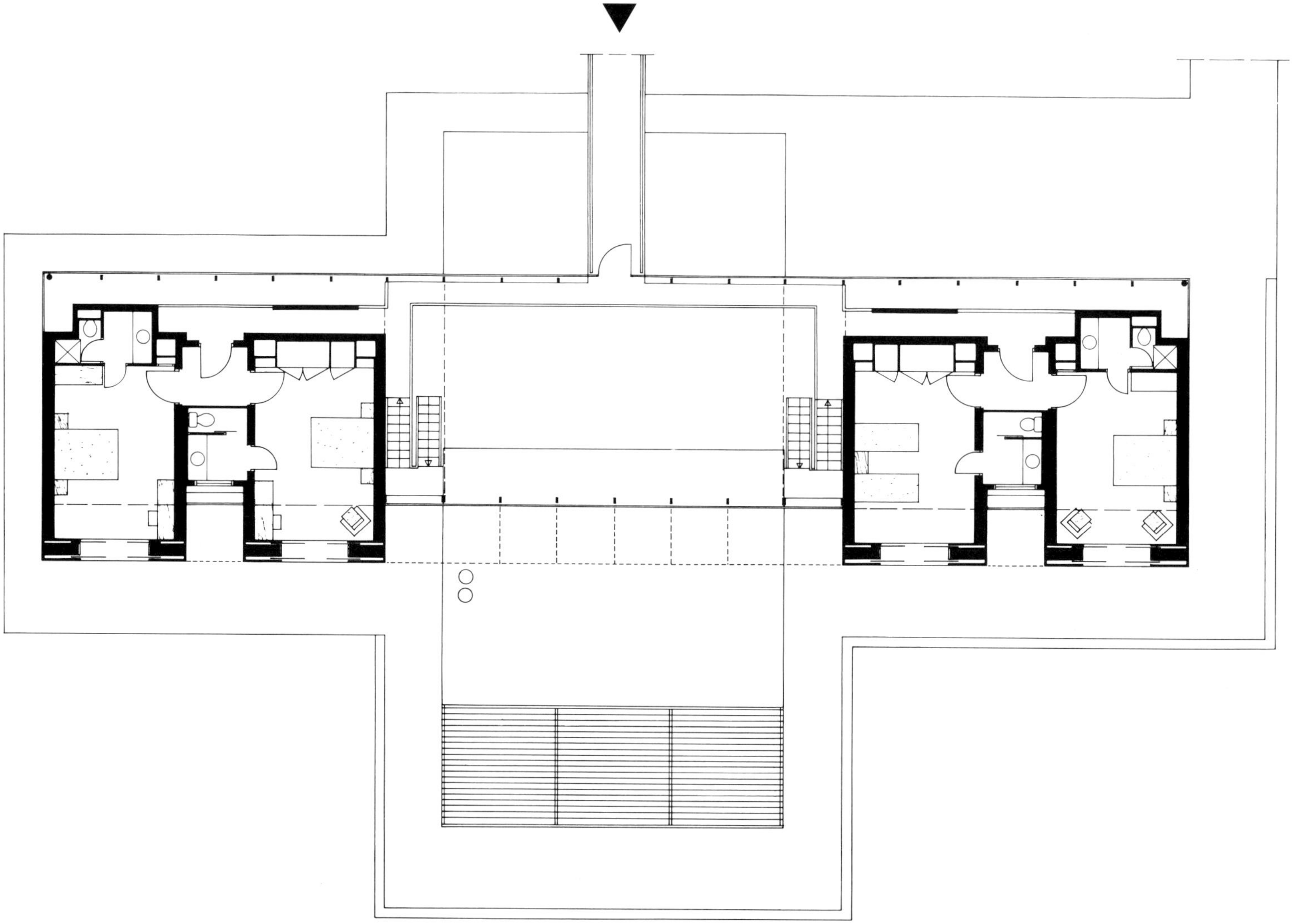

Plan of the ground floor of the Séguéla house. Architect: J.- F. Bodin

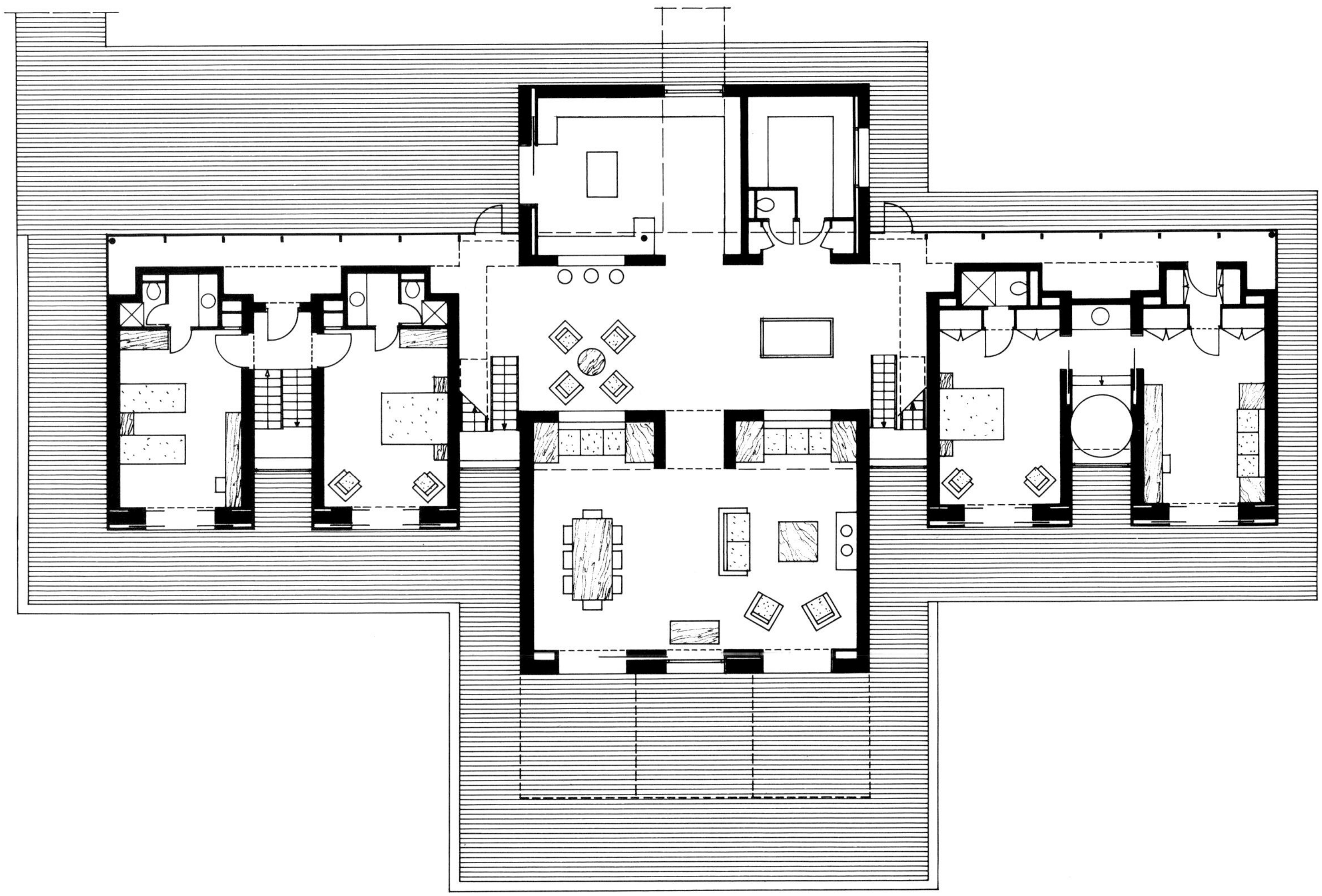

Plan of the upper floor of the Séguéla house.
Architect: J.- F. Bodin

THE OWNER'S DESCRIPTION

First of all, the memories.
All the beaches of the world, all the oceans.
The blues of the Pacific, the emerald of the Bahamas, the smooth white sands, the evening breezes with magenta-coloured clouds, the flotsam and jetsam, the driftwood thrown up by the sea, an epic shipwreck, a message from Robinson Crusoe.
Then the fantasies.
Treasure Island, Jules Verne, the discovery of dream homes in the early American movies, this desire for inviolate peace, the light of *A summer of '42*, the Kennedys at Hyannis Port, the wharves of *Key Largo*, the house at Key West, the endless daydreams about an all-wood house, and the buried memory of the izba, the log house of my origins.
And then the men.
First of all, Jacques and Guy Dewez, who conceived of Sperone.
Xavier, deep blue-eyed prince of Sperone, who emerged from an arbutus more beautiful than any Japanese bonsai, pointed a finger drawn by Michelangelo, and said: "It's here!"
And the architect, Breton, as demanding as a sharp pencil, precise as a compass, who listens so well and so painfully to the owner, and gradually designs the reality.
Then Italo, who operates with an intuition sharper than any electronic device; the master of the red cedar, who—with a curse in Portuguese, Italian and Arabic—can construct a frame, put up a wall, create the perfect doorway.
And then, one day, the house was there.
People say the house resembles me, and yet it is sometimes so beautiful that I still don't always recognize it. It was ready for Her, for Them, just in time. She, the house, is called Treize (Thirteen), a fitting name.

JEAN FELDMAN

THE FELDMAN HOUSE
ARCHITECTS: GEA

The influence of Charles Moore's Sea Ranch development on the architects of Sperone was both direct and indirect. Jean-Marc Roques had worked in Charles Moore's office, and he, Guy André, Guy Breton and Boguslaw Brzeczkowski had also worked together at Avoriaz, an Alpine ski village set in the Savoie, before forming GEA (Groupement d'études architecturales), based in Paris. GEA has been the main architectural firm for Sperone since the mid-1960s. Their office copy of the Charles Moore monograph is by now well-used, but there are important differences between Moore's approach and that of GEA. First, French building standards are much more strict than those for American holiday homes. This has led to higher design standards, further encouraged by the Dewez brothers' insistence that the houses had to be built for year-round occupation. Second, GEA has worked with Canadian red cedar for twenty-five years. This experience led to a much greater technical competency in designing with the material: this is particularly clear in the handling of roof planes and interior spaces.

The Sea Ranch, like Avoriaz, indirectly influenced the Dewez brothers by providing convincing evidence that a true architectural style in timber could be achieved. The influence of Sea Ranch can also be seen in some aspects of the weatherboarding, the constructional details (though this vocabulary has also been developed further at Sperone than in California), and in the importance of finish. And the influence can be seen in the Feldman house, where, as if proof were needed, a photograph of the Calloway house and several drawings of Sea Ranch by M. Feldman hang beside his fireplace.

It is no coincidence that the Feldman house overlooks the thirteenth hole on the golf course,

The house from the sea

Overall view of the house
(in the background,
another house under
construction)

Main and guest room plans of the Feldman house.
Architects: GEA

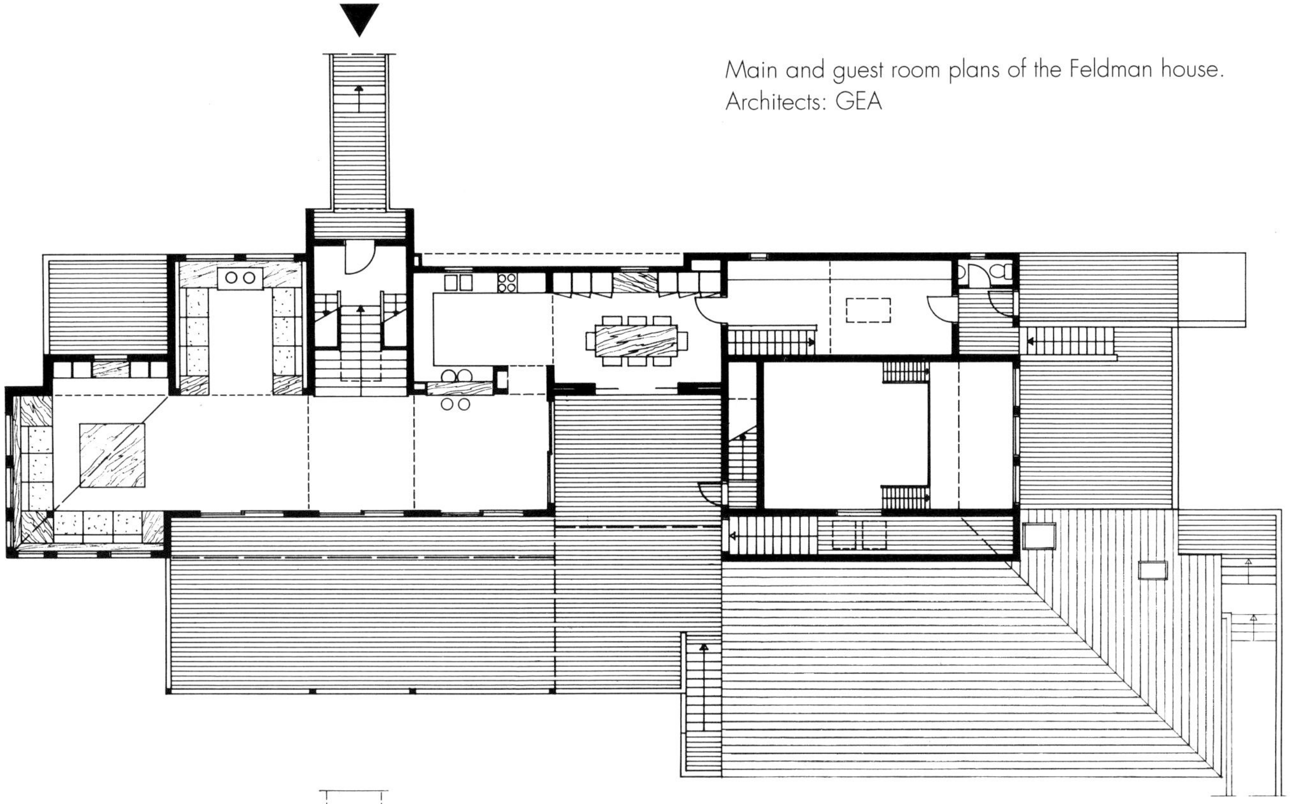

Upper level

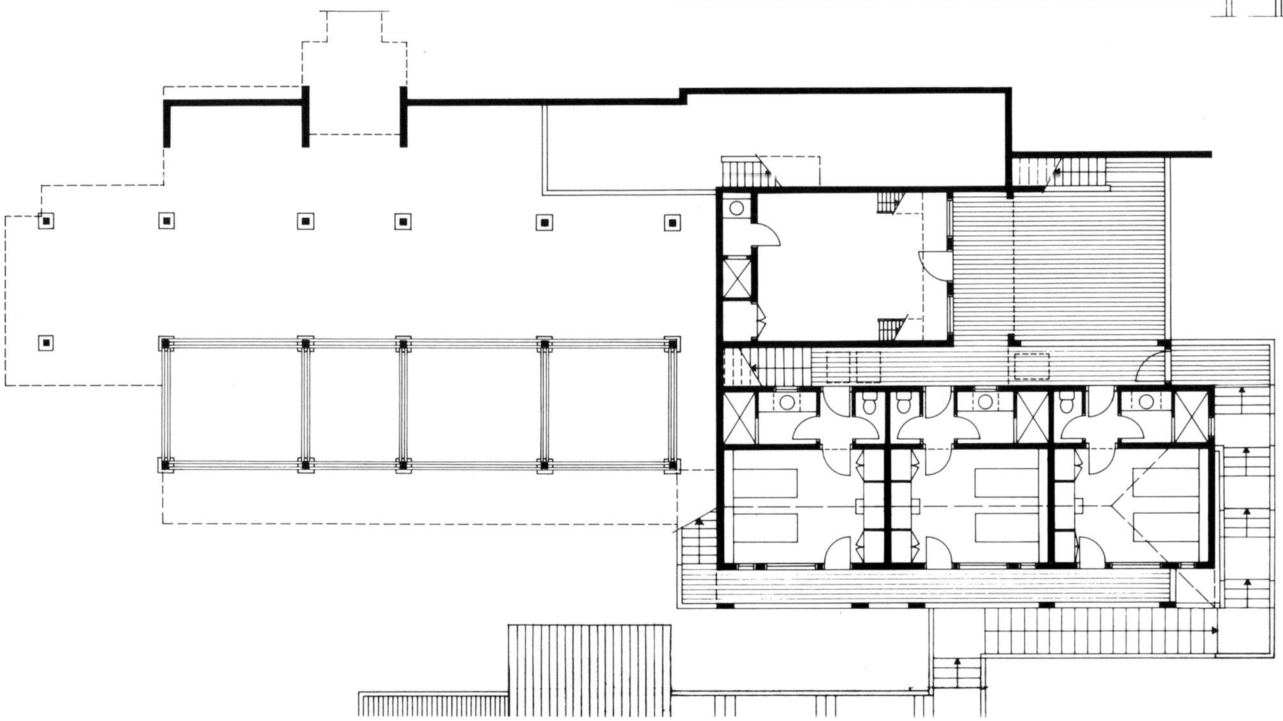

Lower level

The entrance stairway

and occupies lot number thirteen on the general site plan. According to Guy Breton, "Monsieur Feldman is the best kind of clients—he knows clearly what he wants to achieve, but lets the architect find the means to this." Jean Feldman also pays tribute to Breton's care and perspicacity, and his ability to work alongside his client. Feldman developed his own vision of architecture through travel and literature, and spent a long time considering what a house on a coast should be.

Like the Calloway house, which presents an uncompromisingly blank wall on the inland side, one principal feature of the Feldman house is its sweeping exterior wall, which is broken only by a simple doorway and pedimented overlight. Unlike some other buildings at Sperone, where the wood has been stained or painted, the red cedar of the Feldman exterior has been left to weather naturally by the sun and sea winds.

The result is a remarkably stark exterior. The wood, weathered almost black in places,

The living room

The master bedroom

clearly defines spaces and areas. The overall effect reminded me of the samurai castles in Kurosawa's film *Throne of Blood*. In the Feldman house, the starkness is alleviated by the careful and intelligent proportions of the spaces. The formal appearance becomes a social structure, not an imposed formula. The careful choice and design of window openings, roof angles, steps and stairways refine and enliven the whole.

A flight of stairs leads to the central living space from the main door one floor above. There is a pleasant and seemingly deliberate irony in this echo of a grand staircase leading into a plain white room. A hand-carved seagull floats in the centre of the ceiling, its head towards the sea, its wooden wings gliding gently up and down with the movement of the air. The floor and walls of the main living area are white. Plain white benches are built into the walls of the fireplace area to the left of the stairs, and white worktops and stainless steel doors are used in the kitchen on the other side. In the main space, running the whole length of the main block, white settees are placed around a low white table. Full-length sliding glass doors give onto the open deck opposite the entrance staircase. The pool, carefully aligned with the entrance pediment, is reached by a flight of steps.

Looking up from the pool towards the house, you see the guest wing to the right at an intermediate level. From the pool, in fact, the structure supporting the forward edge of the house and deck are visible: the same ordered rigour that informs the design of the whole house is found in the supports and struts. The guest wing is reached from the main deck via an internal stair, which creates a deep narrow passage running across the landward side of the wing. One of the architects called this "the Chinese street": glimpses of well-lit rooms appear along this mysterious passage. The use of large, square window openings (often the full depth of the wall, and fitted as doors) provides a maximum amount of light. The care taken in the

The "Chinese street"

The Feldman house and pool

placing of openings orders the facade and generates light at the right points in the interior space. Daylight streams into the main living area and the same bright calm is repeated in the master bedrooms above the living area. Visitors have told the owner that the house resembles him, yet he sometimes finds the house so beautiful that he still doesn't recognize it. Indeed, the beauty and order of the house are so riveting that you can forget the presence of the sea.

Detail of the timber-frame structure

THE OWNER'S DESCRIPTION

I came for the first time to southern Corsica in 1951 during a cruise. I discovered paradise: Cavallo, the Lavezzi Islands, Bonifacio. In 1974, I purchased a lot in the Baie de Caldarello (Figari).
When I visited Ciappili with Jacques Séguéla in 1983, I instantly fell in love with Sperone and decided to buy land next to Jean Feldman, who purchased his lot at the same time. In August of 1986, Roselyne and I spent a month visiting at every time of the day and night—with and without moonlight—to see, to understand, to feel the best way to live on this site. Then for six months, from September 1986 to March 1987, we worked with the architect Boguslaw Brzeczkowski to draw up plans for "Chateau Roux". We based them on a few guidelines that were extremely simple in theory, but so very difficult to apply.
Here were our basic principles:
1. A wooden house like those at Ciappili, but on a single level to respect the site and not aggress the environment.
2. A wooden house on a single level, but on a large wooden deck, so that once on the deck, you are no longer in contact with the ground, but only with nature (sea and vegetation), something like a boat.
3. A wooden house, something like a boat, in order to have the widest possible view of the sea. In other words, the maximum number of rooms facing the sea; and inside, a living room angled at 45° for a panoramic view from any spot in the living room, kitchen, dining room.
4. A wooden house, something like a boat, with a chimney to sit in front of and still have a view of the sea.
5. A wooden house on a wooden deck, surrounded by a wooden fence so that once past the wooden gate, you turn your back on the rest of the domain; all that remains is a view of the sea, the Lavezzi Islands and Sardinia.

6. A wooden house, to visit in the winter as well as in the summer with a large family—therefore a main living room with, on the port side, an area for the children; and on the starboard, an area for parents and guests.
7. A wooden house on the outside as well as on the inside with simple, high-quality decoration and equipment, made to last—and not to break down like on a boat.
8. A wooden house because wood has the best telluric characteristics.
And because "I like the sound of bodies at night in the midst of woods".

BERNARD ROUX

Overall view of the Roux house and (above) the patio entrance

The Roux house

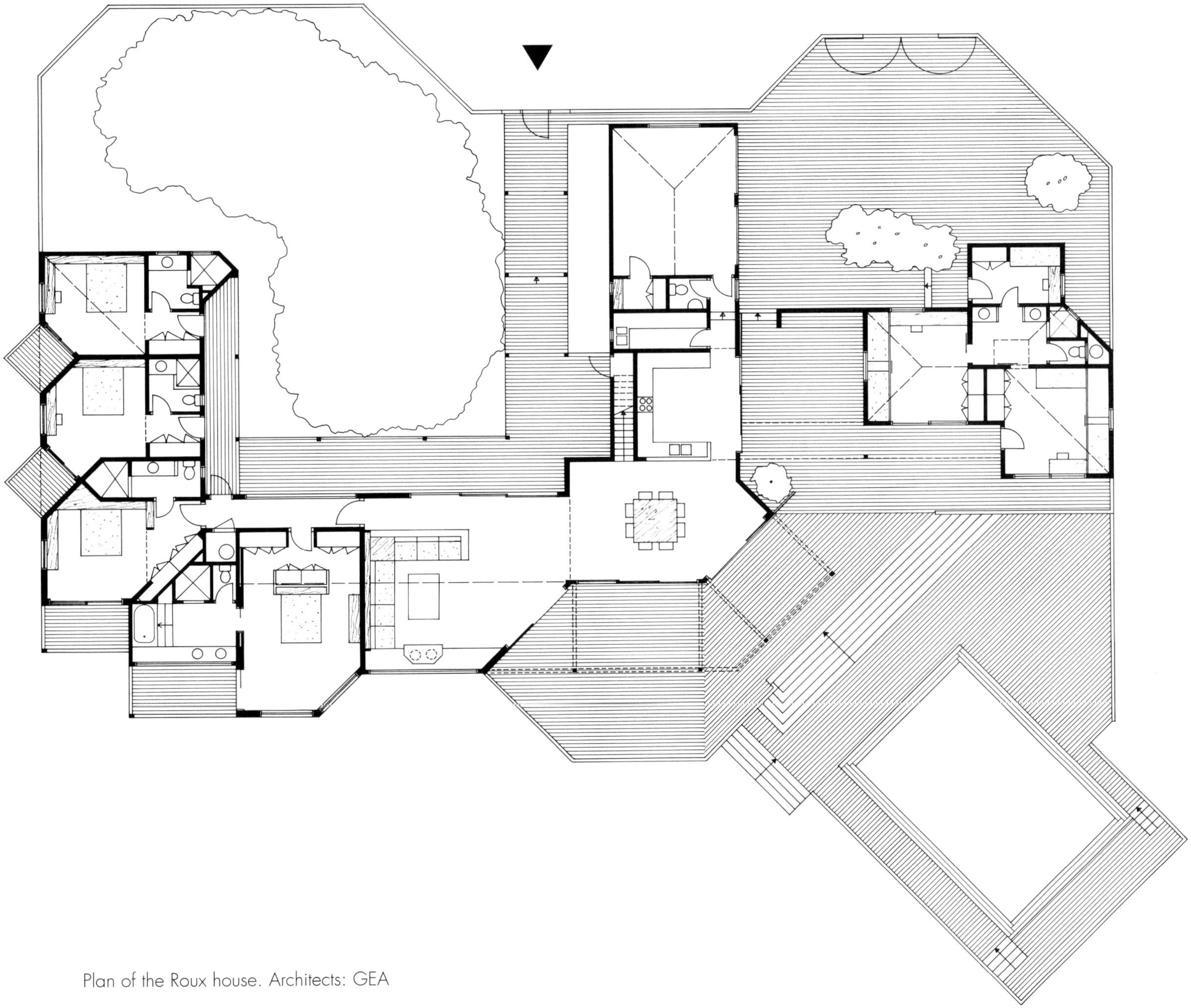

Plan of the Roux house. Architects: GEA

THE ROUX HOUSE
ARCHITECTS: GEA

Jacques Séguéla told me that some of his colleagues had baptized Sperone "Medialand", because of the number of people from advertising, television and journalism who have bought or built houses there. Séguéla himself is proud that he encouraged many of them to consider Sperone, after inviting them to his own homes. But the rather tacky idea of "Wardour Street on the Sea" that the term Medialand suggests is quite out of place. All those who have built there have done so in a way that has respected the environment and the essence of Sperone. This is particularly true of the Roux house, which sits on the outward flank of the Hauts de Sperone, next to the Feldman house.

As M. Roux explains in his own text, it was the sea that initially led him to southern Corsica. For his own house at Sperone, therefore—created with Brzeczkowski of GEA—the sea was to remain a constant metaphor. The house is built on one level, with a continuous exterior deck facing the sea. It sweeps round in a bowed shape, so that the view changes as the visitor moves from the guest wing across the entrance area—with a large outdoor dining table—past the kitchen to the main indoor living space. This space is also angled to follow the contour of the coast, and consists of a large room with a vast fireplace at one end and full-length glazed doors that create a window onto the deck, the *maquis* and the sea. The bedrooms are situated around an inner court behind the living area. The principal idea was to ensure a panoramic view over the sea. As the whole house overlooks the *maquis*, the sea immediately seems to be closer, as from the deck of a ship.

This nautical metaphor is heightened by the pale, weathered grey of the painted external woodwork. Inside, white gloss paint has been used throughout, together with whitewood furniture. If the defining characteristics of

the Mediterranean coast are sea, sun and simplicity, then the Roux house fits the bill well enough. It is clearly a house designed as a vantage point onto sea and land, elegantly proportioned and neatly fitted out, like the schooner that first brought Michel Roux to the Straits of Bonifacio.

The deck offers a panoramic view over the sea and the *maquis*

Two views of the living
room; there is no real
separation between
interior and exterior

The master bedroom (above) and the stairs leading to the pool

The Roux house from
the pool

THE OWNER'S DESCRIPTION

The design of our house at Sperone meets a certain number of conditions that for many years have been linked to our ecological vision of architecture, the use of materials and the occupation of space.

For us, architecture must be practical and unique, even daring on the inside, while discreet and mimetic on the outside.

The decision to use the architects of GEA, which designed the Ciappili development, coincided with our desires. It was these architects who, twenty years ago, constructed our wooden house bordering a forest in Normandy.

The choice of material—wood—also coincides with an ecological decision. Wood best fits the site, but above all, it is a renewable resource, as opposed to stone, concrete or any other material made from fossil resources, which require a great deal of energy to produce. Furthermore, wood is alive and warm. It moves, cracks, speaks with the elements and makes a house as solid as an oak, yet as flexible as a reed.

As for respecting the landscape, a wooden house is a necessary prerequisite, but it is not enough. The layout, in relation to the site and in relation to other houses, is also a determining factor. In this respect, the zoning plan for the Sperone domain is a success, even a model. It complies with our requirement to have a house that fits into the landscape, not as an intruder, but as a friend.

Added to this is the pleasure of living in a house that clings to the cliff, that is designed for a "variable" family where we can all be together or in separate areas without getting in each other's way. You sense that the architect and the contractor—whose skill and imagination are remarkable—enjoyed building this house.

LOUIS BÉRIOT

THE BÉRIOT HOUSE
Architects: GEA

Of all the houses on the inner flank of the Hauts de Sperone, the Bériot house is perhaps in the most dramatic setting. From the roadside, a wooden fence some six feet high blocks any view of the house, and even the wooden walkway from the entrance door only begins to suggest the daring of the house. The walkway ends in a deck, with a guest wing to one side, the main living area to the other, the golf course and the sea beyond in front. And below, a steep drop of about a hundred feet to the edge of the golf course. Like a swallow's nest under the eaves, the Bériot house projects from the escarpment.

A sliding glass door leads from the deck into the living space: at the back is a small kitchen, with a breakfast bar and dining area. There is then a step down into the seating area. Broad, white canvas-covered seats are fitted into the wooden frame of the house. A side window overlooks the inner flank of the Hauts de Sperone, while a canted bay window drops down through the floor to bring light to the room below. This device reinforces the drama of the house's position and brings the surrounding landscape much closer. The narrowness of the central window panel also emphasizes the almost vertiginous view downwards.

A similar window is found in the main bedroom on the opposite side of the deck. On the lower level, there is a rather nautical bedroom fitted out with bunks at the back, and a study/bedroom at the front. With a desk filling the window embrasure, the room serves as M. Bériot's workroom: he is a writer on environmental and architectural matters. Seeing this small, calm room with its astonishing views reminded me of Burton Rascoe's remark that "a writer is working even when he's looking out of the window".

Many of the houses at Sperone react to breezes or winds with an occasional gentle

The deck from the living room

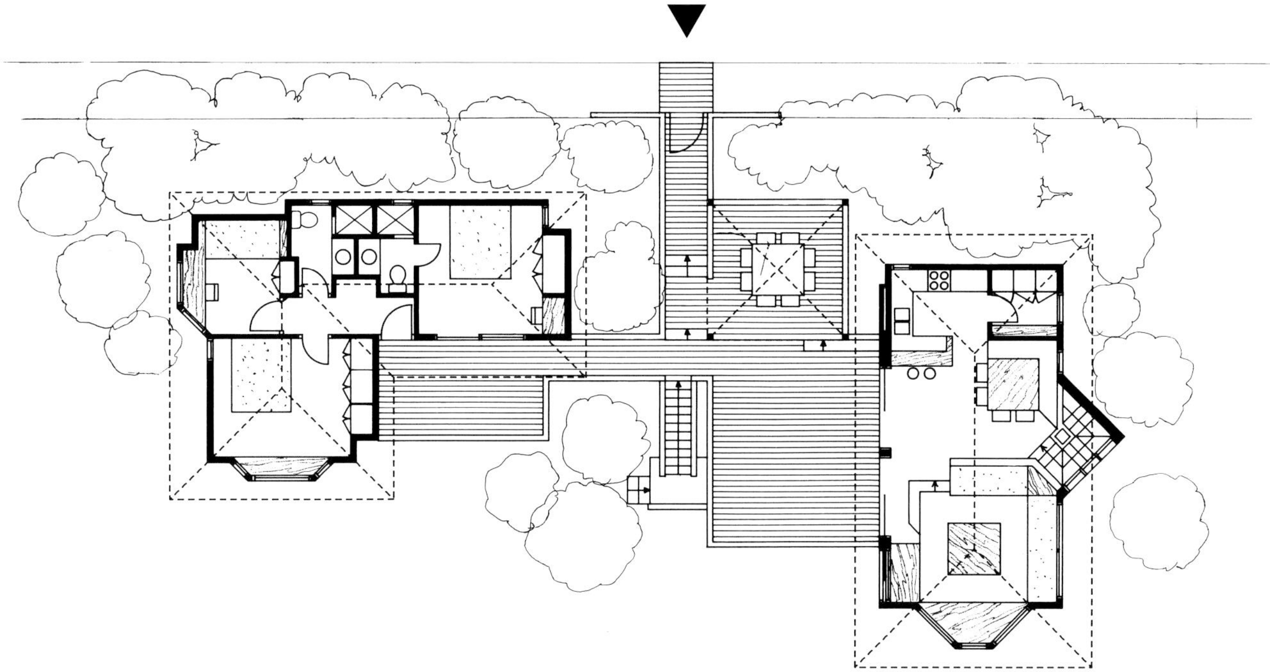

Main level

Plans of the Bériot house. Architects: GEA

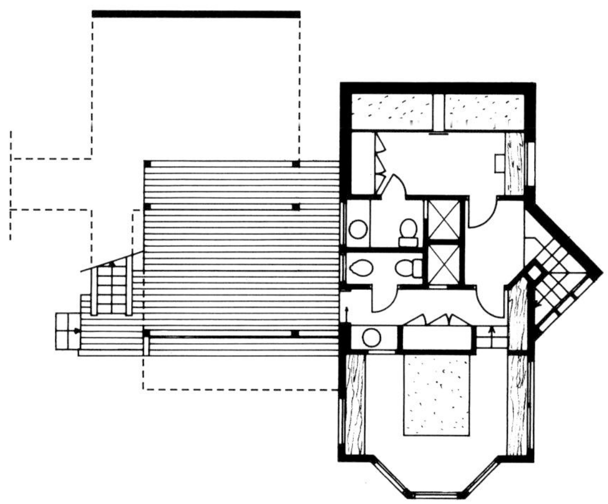

Lower level

movement, and a creak of timber (though none has ever succumbed to the fierce winter storms that hammer the southern coast of Corsica). The outside decks often thrum and vibrate under passing feet. But in the Bériot house, one is particularly aware of being linked to the landscape, part of a wider process in which wood, the most natural of building materials, plays an essential role. This was an essential requirement for Louis and Catherine Bériot. They had already worked with Guy Breton of GEA some twenty years before to build a house in a forest in Normandy, and saw at Sperone the opportunity to create a house that would be ecologically non-invasive, and constructed from renewable source materials. Their confident and daring statement makes for one of the most exciting houses at Sperone.

The Bériot house, for example, is unusual in that the supporting framework is visible because it does not have insulating inner walls. Designed for simplicity, this solution in no way diminishes the architectural interest of the house. Indeed, it proves that houses with different budgets can coexist perfectly well and even enhance each other.

The Bériot house, as the accompanying photographs show, highlighted one of the main problems of photographing the endlessly changing patterns, movement and levels of light at Sperone. Early morning starts were often needed, Richard Bryant recalls, despite the hazards of the automatic watering system on the golf course, and the natural impenetrability of the maquis! And only too often there would be only one moment for the right image before the shadows altered with the passage of the sun. We deliberately tried to use artificial light as little as possible, as the first reconnaissance visit to Sperone instantly revealed the importance of using natural light, not only in linking the houses to the landscape, but also in the architectural conception of the houses themselves. The midday sun, for example, flattened the contours of the buildings completely, and drew

The living room in daylight
and at night

them back into the surrounding vegetation. Another problem was the flexibility and mobility of the open decks, from which many photographs were taken—they would move slightly under wind pressure or as people walked about.

Of course, these qualities that posed such a challenge to the photographer were also at the heart of the design of the houses. It is precisely because they are open to the wind and the sun, and at one with their surroundings, rather than imposed on them, that the houses are so successful.

Sunrise and sunset from the deck

The Bériot house lit up at night

THE MICHEL HOUSE
ARCHITECTS: GEA

With the Bériot house, the problem posed by the escarpment is solved by arranging the rooms in a vertical stack. The Michel house is slightly farther away along the ridge. Here the architect has adopted a different solution in terms of the slope, by making use of a spur running into the nearby escarpment. Instead of piling the rooms into a single unit, as is so elegantly done at the Bériot house, architect and client opted for a series of independent guest pavilions. So at the level of the main roadway, there is an entrance area with a completely enclosed internal garden; adjoining this are the main living area, kitchen, living room and main bedroom, which face the pool. Because of the steep slope, the end of the pool is almost projecting into the void. The guest bedrooms, each with their own bathroom and terrace, form a series of smaller pavilions linked by walkways to the main house. Three of these pavilions drop down the side of the hill one after another, much like a mother hen with a flock of chicks behind her.

The exterior of the house has been left unfinished, and presents, as do so many houses at Sperone, different tints and colours according to the varying degrees of sunlight and shade. In the interior, a different range of colours has been used. Inside the main living area, the exposed carpentry of the ceilings has been painted white, and a plain wood floor has been laid. This is set off with wooden tables, cupboards, and rattan armchairs, while chrome steel chairs are used in the dining area. The kitchen, which overlooks the pool at the angle of the house, has been finished in dark grey; tall chrome steel stools create a bar area around the central cooking point, which is finished in brushed steel and aluminium, giving a rather serious and fiercely practical air to the whole room.

In the main living area, however, the atmosphere of clear serenity created by the plain pale wood is heightened by the glassware displayed on the cupboard shelving, together with a collection of mounted butterflies and moths in glass cases. This is one of the houses at Sperone where a formal decorative element runs through the internal layout. More often we find the atmosphere of a holiday home, the rooms busy with objects which clearly have their own place, but are arranged according to a theme unique to each family.

The kitchen

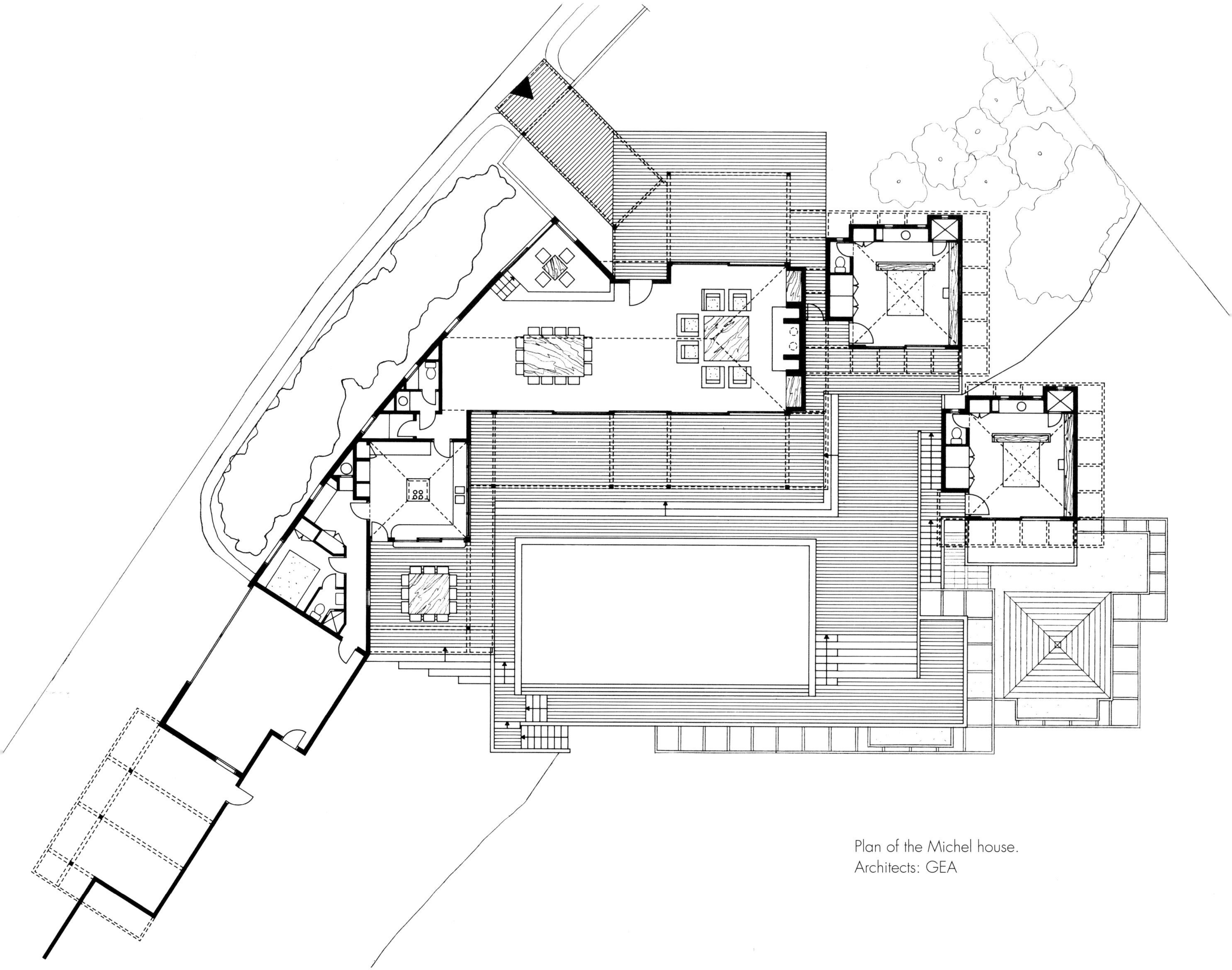

Plan of the Michel house.
Architects: GEA

This front view of the Michel house shows how it hugs the hillside—the living room in the upper part extends to the bedrooms that cascade down the slope.

The Michel house. In the background, the coast of Sardinia

The deck and pool

The master bedroom

The living room

FALATTE

The Pommereau house. In the background, on the left, the F. 6 house

The development at Falatte is the final stage of the middle development at Sperone. The ground slopes gently up from the golf course towards the road bordering the domain and the houses have a view across the course to the sea. Falatte doesn't offer the same opportunity for architectural acrobatics as do the valley at Ciappili or the escarpment at the Hauts de Sperone. This may explain why the plots are considerably larger; indeed, some of the biggest houses at Sperone are found here.

Though quite a number of the homeowners at Sperone work in the media, in television or in advertising, many are also professional and business people. Thus, they do not form a homogenous group. Indeed, Bruno Allais has pointed out how each area tends to develop a slightly different culture, but this is probably due to the length of time each area has been settled. There is, however, one rough generalization that can be made about Falatte: many of the owners have taken advantage of the larger sites to create houses with more elaborate interior designs. The proximity of the *maquis* and the sea views at Ciappili and the Hauts de Sperone seem to compensate for the relatively modest interior decoration. At Falatte, however, there seems to be a keener interest in comfort and elegance within.

This is not a comment on quality: all the interior decoration of houses on the domain is generally a reflection of the range of taste, travel and sophistication of the owners, and shows judgement and reflection. Indeed, just as the seeming similarities of the architecture at Sperone diverge on closer view into a myriad of original individual solutions, so it is with interior decoration. There are common themes—sailing and the sea, not surprisingly, are examples. But the forms in which such themes are expressed vary widely, demonstrating the breadth of wit and intelligence inspiring the designs.

The Sperone domain, as we have seen, is an architectural project of the highest quality; there

are few other holiday or leisure sites worldwide with the same attention to the environment, to architectural detail, to lifestyle. But the whole effect is carefully understated to permit the natural beauty of the site to permeate the buildings and lifestyle of the domain.

THE POMMEREAU HOUSE
ARCHITECTS: GEA

While the development at Falatte shares with the rest of the domain an orientation both towards the sea to one side and the *maquis* on the other, the slopes are gentler, and there is less opportunity to build on many different levels. The Pommereau house elegantly meets the challenge of an almost horizontal site by facing towards the sea and by incorporating a garden within the perimeter of the house.

The floor plan shows how the guest rooms on the northern side of the house are stepped back to give each one a view down to the sea; each one also has a private decked area separate from the main house (a motif used for the master bedroom as well). The back bedroom has a view inland and a view towards the sea over the interior garden. This garden, open to the sky, sits on the dividing line between the main and guest areas of the house. The main block comprises the living area, kitchen and main bedroom. The owner's taste for pictures, contemporary furniture and crafts animates the interiors, and each guest room has a different style and colour scheme. The game room at the back of the house, for example, uses traditional Corsican motifs in black on white as a design theme. Within the main room, the two steel tension wires contribute to the design by doubling up as wiring for the low-voltage light system.

Although the house is built on a single level, the horizon line is a constant reference. In the bathroom off the main bedroom, the bath itself has been raised to give the user a clear view out to sea. Outside, the pool is set slightly below the level of the house, so that the water appears to merge with the sea beyond. On the exterior, the roof overhangs often found on the houses of the domain have disappeared. The external walls rise to hide the roof edges, and the rooftops are visible above them, enclosed by the top ridge of the walls. Horizontal sunscreens provide shade over the deck area and around the garden. This element, and the cheerful magnolia cream colour in which the outside is painted, creates a toylike charm: it is difficult to

The deck off the living room and steps leading to the garden

Entrance to the house

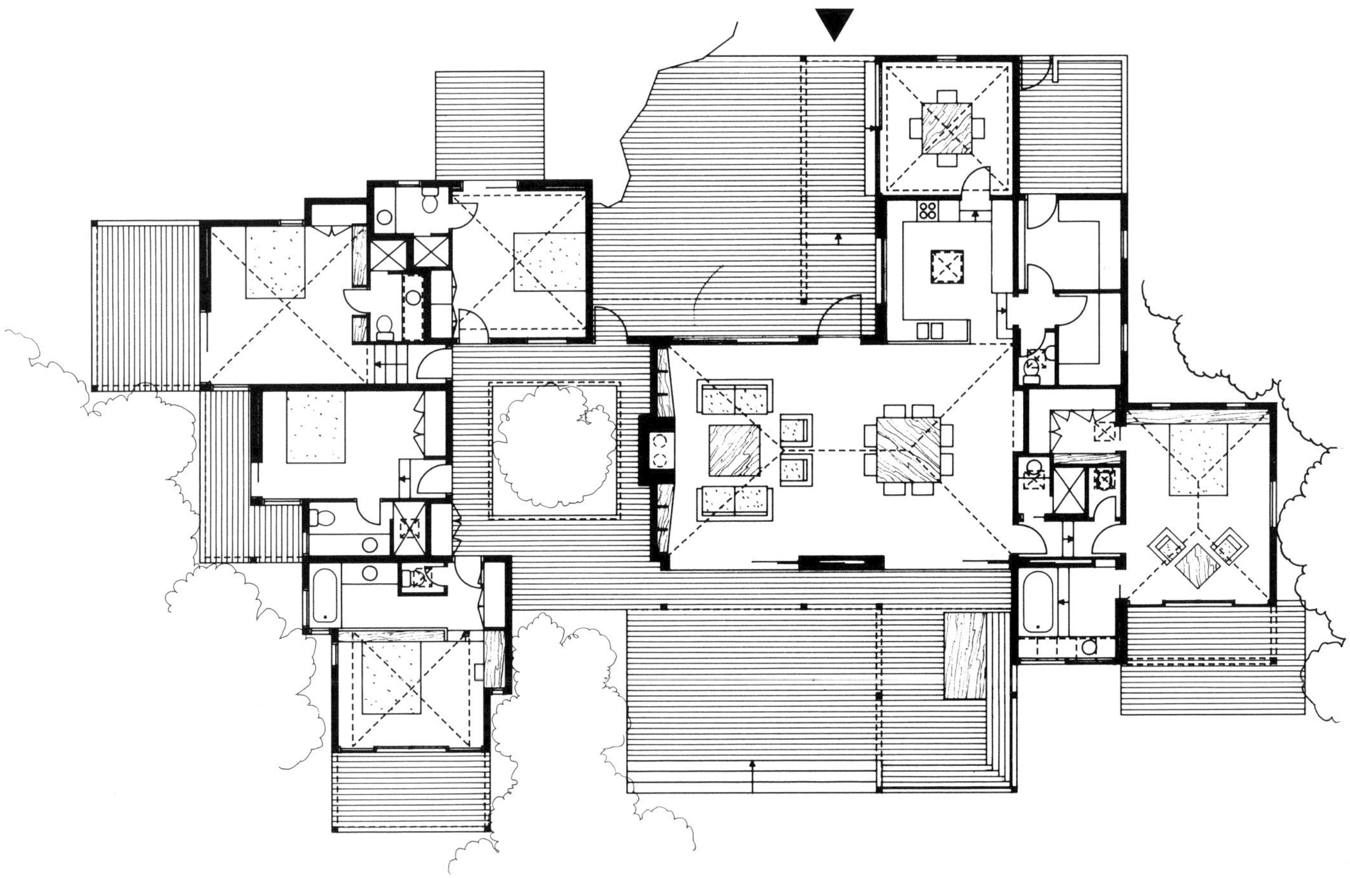

Plan of the Pommereau house. Architects: GEA

View of the main deck

imagine that this is actually a very solid house.

The idea of hiding the roof edges created an interesting design problem for Brzeczkowski, the job architect for the Pommereau house. It was important that all the roof profiles be similar, and that the smaller individual roofs be visually equivalent in size. This meant putting flat roofing over some of the intermediate spaces, while at the same time ensuring that the roofs over individual rooms—the guest rooms, for example—were also centred on the rooms. According to Brzeczkowski, the roof structures at Sperone were habitually the most challenging aspects of a design. They had to fit around the often complex floor plans and be part of the interior spaces, since few houses at Sperone have suspended ceilings. The Pommereau house, with its gentle and welcoming mood, is one of the most successful and unusual resolutions of this problem.

The living room with the metallic tie rods which are also used as low-voltage conductors

The master bathroom

Guest bedroom

The living room

THE OWNER'S DESCRIPTION

In a country of wind and light, facing an endless panorama, we wanted to create a house that offers different landscapes and a multitude of lighting.
We therefore opted for a "screen house", where the rejection of straight lines creates—through the various roofs, diagonals and right angles—a constant effect of surprise.
We were inspired by the desire to integrate the house into the all-powerful *maquis*, and to protect it from the prevailing winds.
To balance the contemporary appearance, flexibility and lightness of wood, we wanted to use solid materials such as tiling, glass mosaic, azulejos, and stone (the ciappe of the chimney), all souvenirs from our travels.
The Polynesian influence and its art de vivre motivated our decision to create separate houses (farés), radiating from the central core created by the patio. This enclosed patio is structured by its columns, which reflects a Spanish/Moorish influence.
A basin in the middle holds the water that flows from the fountain.
This house "of many influences" successfully solves the difficult challenge of combining an unlimited view facing an exceptional landscape with an intimacy that protects those who live within.

FRANCIS and PASCALE CHAPUS

THE CHAPUS HOUSE
ARCHITECT: FRANCIS CHAPUS

The architectural vocabulary was forged at Ciappili, then further developed and refined at the Hauts de Sperone. The houses at Falatte, however, were constructed after the battles had been won. The architects could therefore adopt a more relaxed and independent view. This evolution is best represented by one of the most unusual houses at Falatte, the Chapus house. Its original and eclectic style shows just how far the construction principles devised at Sperone could be stretched to include different ideas. Monsieur Chapus, himself an architect, and his wife created a house that fully reflected their own tastes.

The porch over the main deck

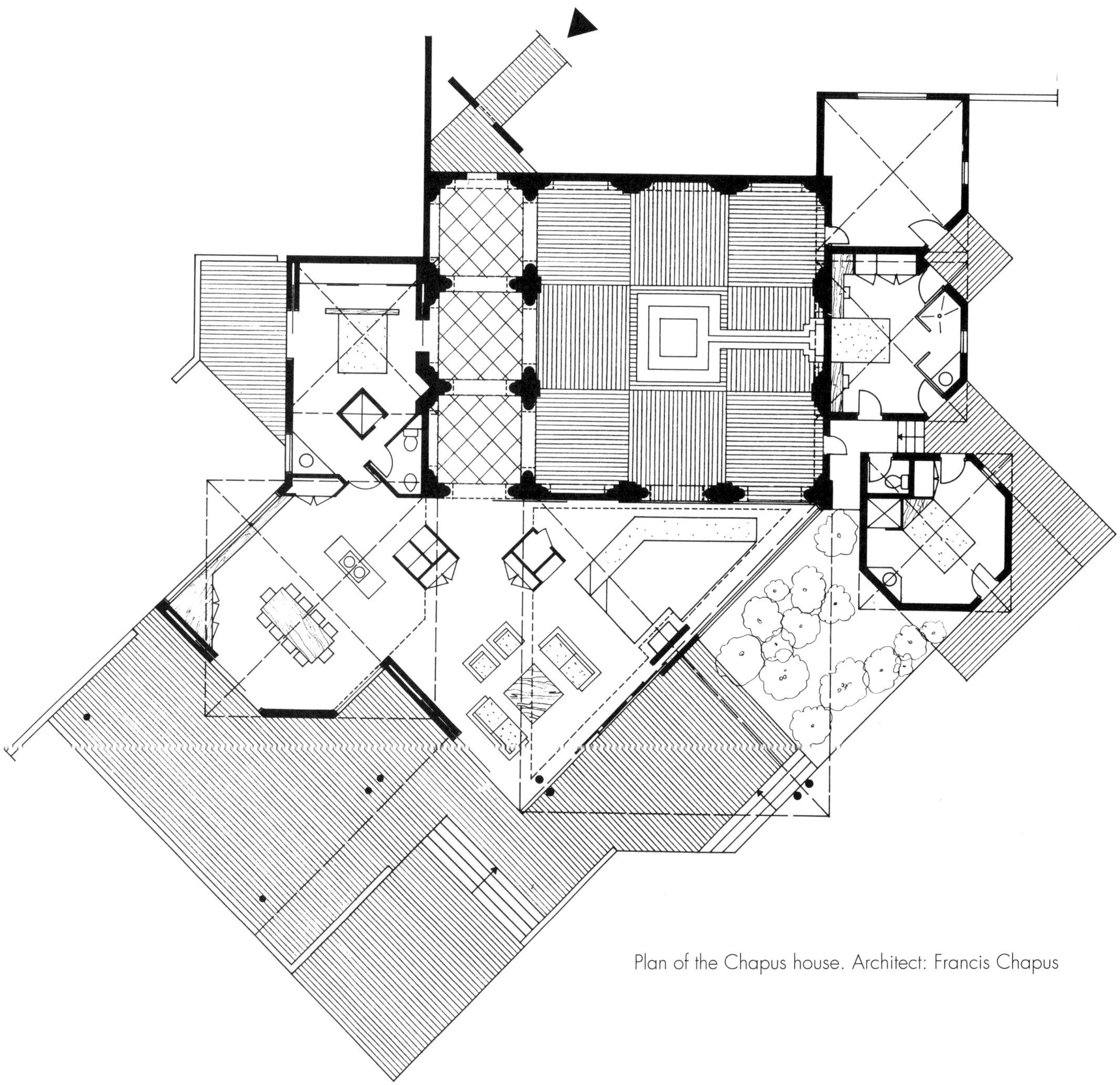

Plan of the Chapus house. Architect: Francis Chapus

The patio portico

The patio

The floor plan for the Chapus house shows the same cheerful disregard for rectilinear design first achieved at Ciappili. But the house is on one storey only (as are many houses on the gentler slopes at Falatte), and quietly rejects the fusion between the interior and the exterior that is common at Sperone by creating an enclosed, Moorish-style interior courtyard in the centre of the house. This design motif, according to the owner, recalls the work of Frank Lloyd Wright, one of the greatest architects of the twentieth century, who often incorporated diverse architectural styles into contemporary designs.

Dining area in the
Chapus house

THE F. 6 HOUSE
ARCHITECTS: GEA

As we have seen, the landscape at Falatte is more conducive to long, low houses, and the F. 6 house is no exception. Apart from a main bedroom superimposed over the main block, the rest of the house is laid out in a single line, facing the golf course towards the sea. One notable feature is the swimming pool, situated along the main axis of the house, which creates, as at the Pommereau house, a trompe-l'œil effect on its outer edge—the water of the pool seems to disappear directly into the horizon of the sea beyond.

Within the house itself—which is finished in wood stained in slightly differing shades of grey and cream to create a varied but coherent interior—the Mediterranean atmosphere has been emphasized by the use of carefully chosen pieces of contemporary furniture. The openwork wrought-iron armchairs and seats, wooden folding tables, and sofas housed in loose canvas coatings in pale striped colours all convey a lightness of touch and a relaxed environment. The central feature of the main living area is the fireplace, where the chimney breast has been faced in dark green marble—a subtle touch of ostentation in an otherwise calm and confident interior. Pierced openwork panels in several internal walls and doors vary the levels of daylight within the house.

The F. 6 house viewed
from the garden

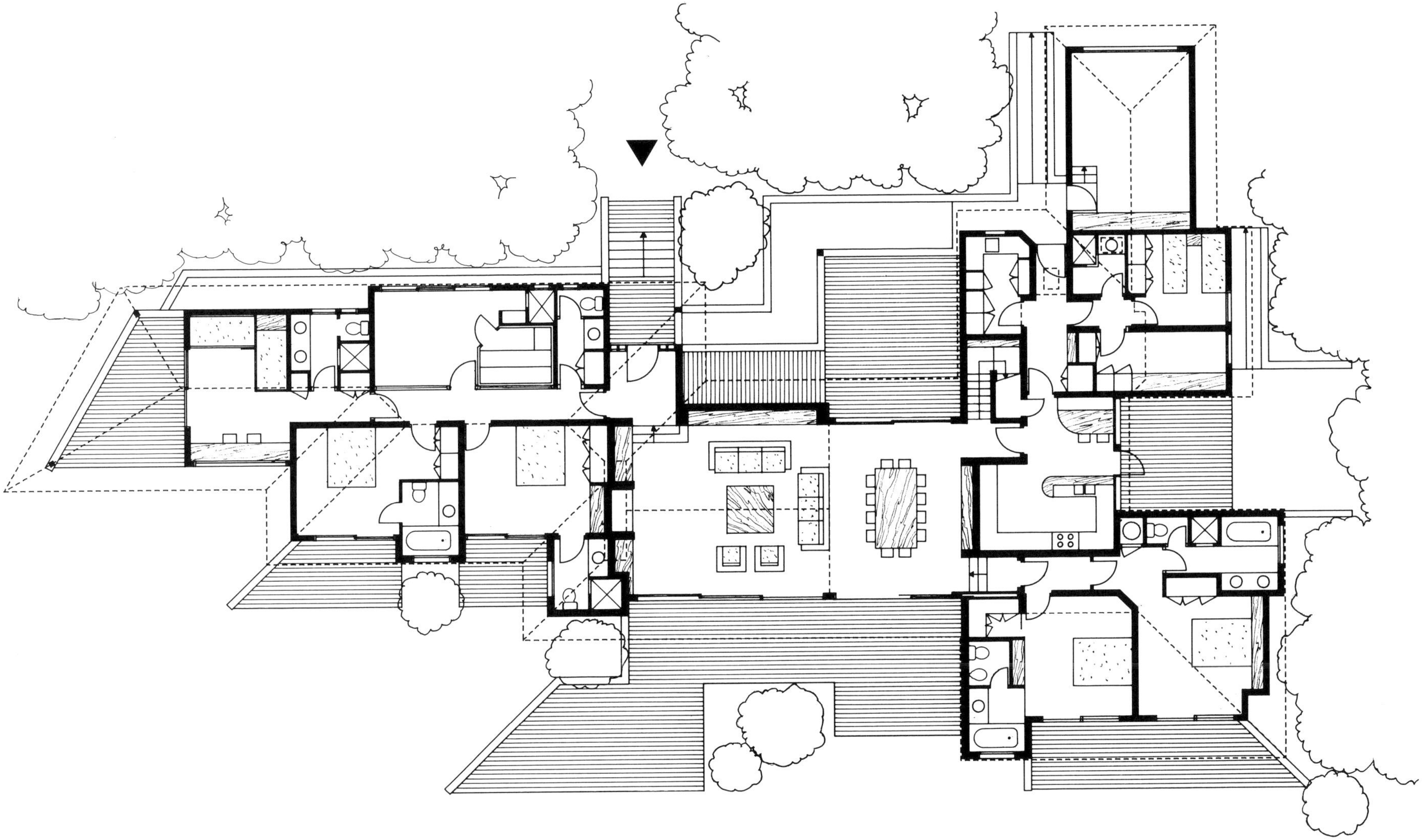

Plan of the main floor of the F. 6 house. Architects: GEA

The study adjoining the master bedroom (upper level)

The living room and
terrace

The pool of the F. 6 house.
Beyond, the islands of the
Lavezzi archipelago and
Sardinia

The master bedroom (above) and detail of the roof

THE GOLF COURSE AND THE CLUB HOUSE

THE CLUB HOUSE
ARCHITECTS: GEA

The golf course at Sperone was developed out of the need to provide a central theme and a recreational facility for the domain, once the idea of a permanent yacht marina was abandoned. The Dewez brothers invited Robert Trent Jones, Sr., an internationally known course designer, to create the 18-hole course, thereby ensuring not only that the layout of greens, fairways and tees would harmonize with the splendid site, but that the quality of the course design would equal that of the domain as a whole. Robert Trent Jones, Sr., fulfilled their expectations magnificently. The course is laid out to the highest international standards, and presents a series of keen tests to golfers. At the sixteenth hole, for example, is a world-class challenge: the player drives towards the fairway from the promontory of the old semaphore station; the ball has to pass over the sea below.

Perhaps the great merit of Sperone is that it revealed to the public the splendour of a heretofore totally unknown site.

The course covers a total of 178 acres, and this creates the right balance between recreation and housing. Bruno Allais estimates that the number of houses on the domain could have been doubled if the golf course had not been built, but this would have deteriorated the quality of life for everyone. In Sardinia, housing has been overdeveloped around golf courses, to the detriment of everyone.

For the domain as a whole, the course has provided a central focus, and the Club House is a social meeting point. In fact, quite a few owners have taken up golf and others have become interested in the game. One owner whose house overlooks the fairway has offered a case of champagne to anyone who can get a ball into his swimming pool in one shot from the nearest tee—to date the prize remains unclaimed.

Two views of the Club House

Lower level access

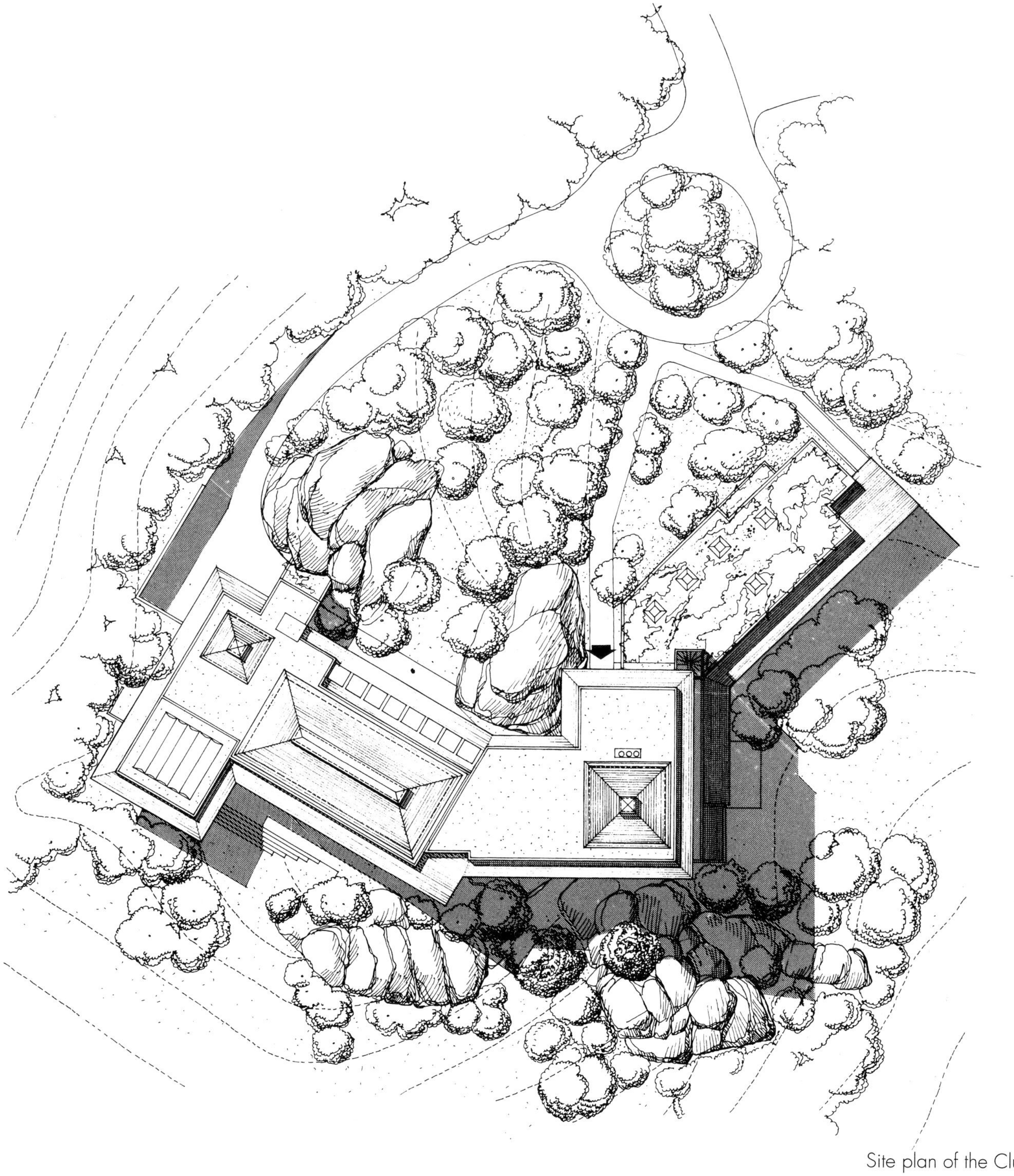

Site plan of the Club House

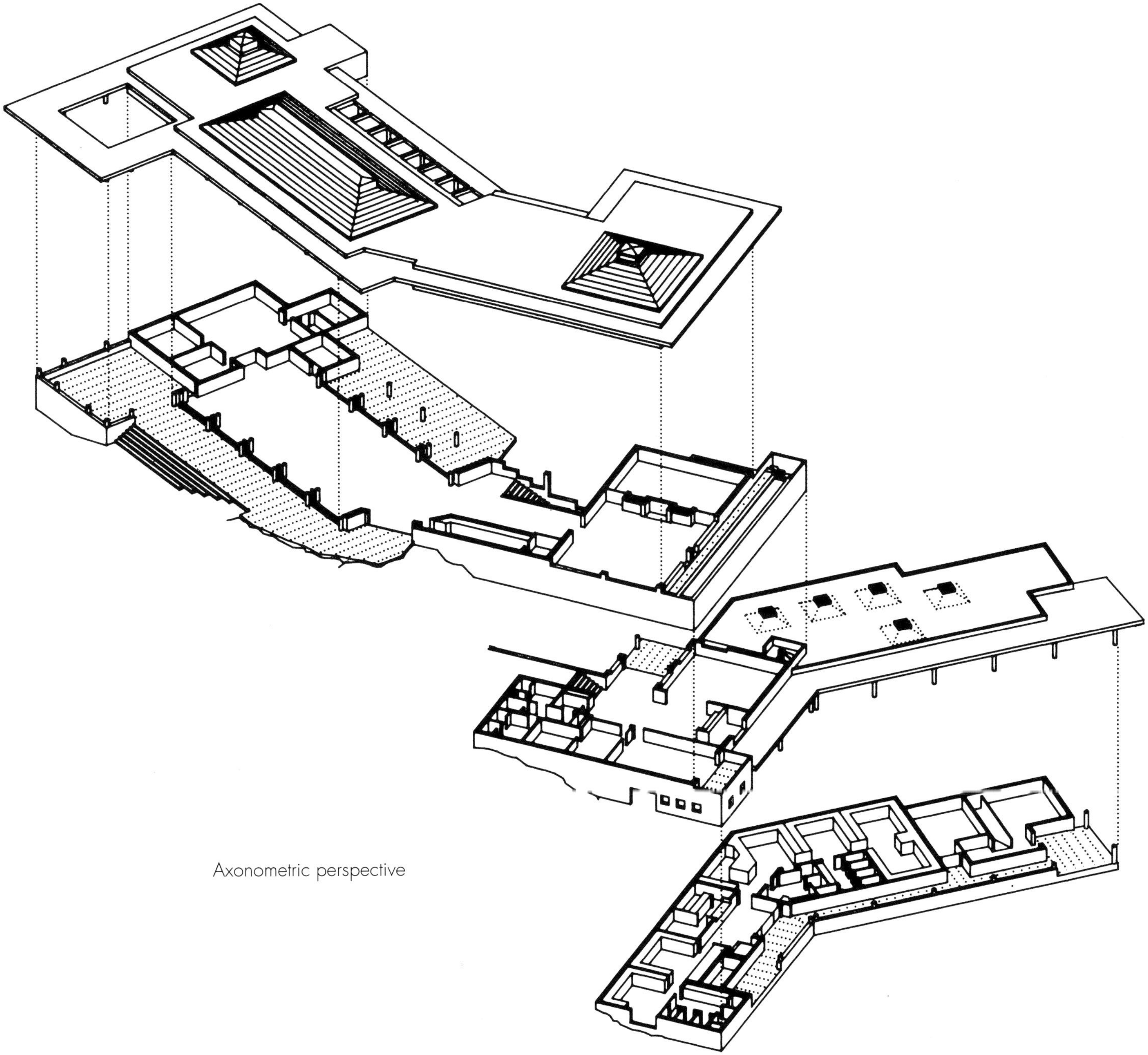

Axonometric perspective

Main entrance to the Club House and (opposite) staircase leading to the bar, restaurant and members' rooms

The golf course has had broader benefits. By no means all the golfers are residents of Sperone, so the course brings additional business to nearby hotels and restaurants. The golfing season is four times longer than the summer tourist season—indeed, one of the reasons for creating the course was to provide a facility that could be used year round. The golf course has exceeded expectations: it is busiest during the "off" season. While eighty percent of the tourist trade is concentrated into July and August, only twenty percent of the golfing turnover is in those months. The course, along with the other tourist facilities, contributes to Dewez's aim of encouraging economic development in the area.

The Club House, the centre of community events and activities, occupies something of a central social position at Sperone. Because it was intended for public rather than private use, the building regulation requirements precluded an exclusively wood structure. A conventional steel frame and concrete-floored structure was therefore designed. This had the added advantage of allowing for subsequent modifications and extensions to meet future demand. And the details are in keeping with the same design vocabulary as the rest of the development, particularly the wood siding used on external walls and the wooden roof tiles.

The Club House is also centrally located on a slight promontory. To the right is the inward flank of the Hauts de Sperone, to the left the houses at Falatte, and beyond them, towards the east, the new apartments at Piantarella. In front of the Club House stretches the practice green and most of the course, and beyond, a fine view of the sea towards Sardinia. The building has three storeys; as it is built on a slope, each one has a level entrance. The entrance is partly hidden by the natural rock outcrop which frames the landward side. The entry hall gives onto the secretary's office, golf shop and reception area. Stairs lead up to the restaurant and bar, and down to the changing rooms; from here, a passage leads to the pro's office and the green-

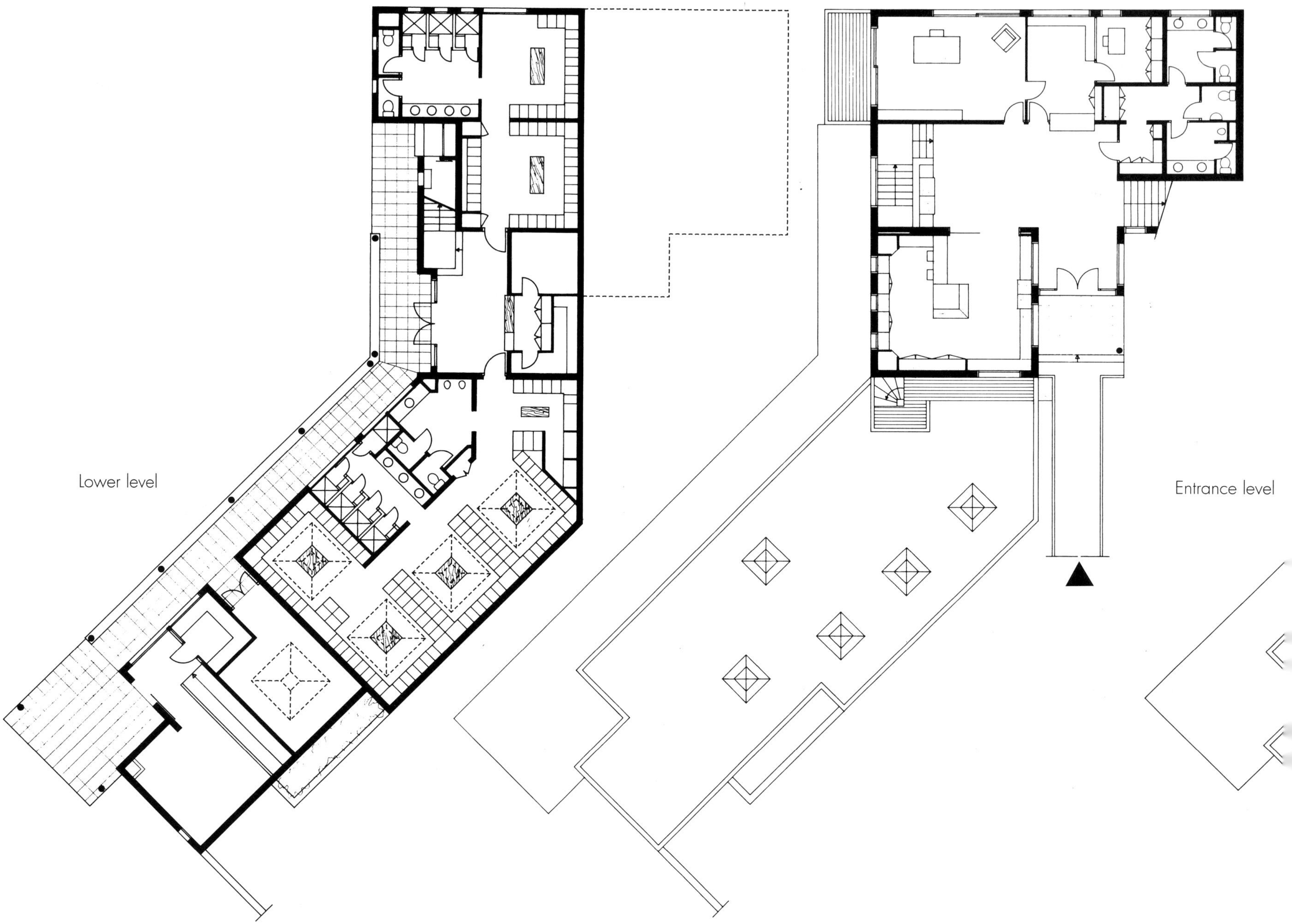

Lower level

Entrance level

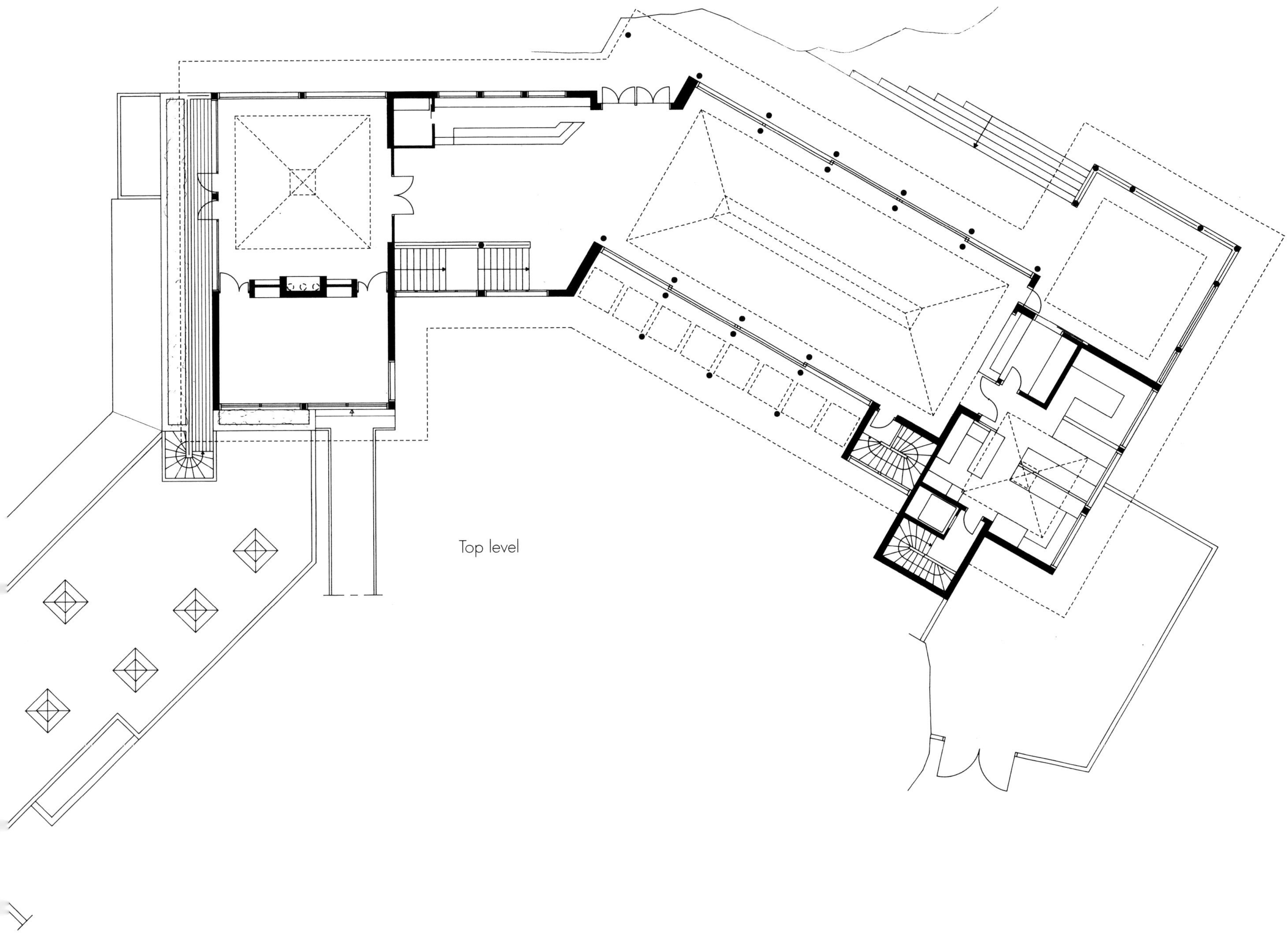

Map of the Club House. Architects: GEA

The bar (above) and the main lounge

The restaurant

keeper's shop. The building contains three linked elements—in the centre, the mezzanine, bar and member's room; to the east, the changing rooms; and to the west, the restaurant and the kitchen level. Because this arrangement follows the natural contour of the hill, the building appears to be on a single storey (except when viewed from the east). It commands excellent views, yet does not dominate the landscape.

At the lower level, the changing rooms are equipped with white lockers and are lit with overhead skylights framed in plain varnished wood. Outside, a covered walkway leads to the offices and to the first tee and practice tee. At the entrance level, large windows on the landward side face the granite outcrop on which the house is built, and broad stairs lead up to the bar, member's room and restaurant. The first two are directly over the entrance area, while the restaurant angles off from the building. From the member's room, there is a view over Falatte, while the bar faces landward. It is furnished with chairs and tables designed by Yves Pochy. The restaurant is a single long room; full-length glass doors along each side lead to terraces. On the landward side, the terrace faces the top of the outcrop, while the other side offers a view over the fairway, *maquis* and sea. At the end of the seaward terrace is a belvedere with an open roof.

The size, function and construction of the Club House make it different from the general run of buildings at Sperone, yet it retains the spirit of the place. The layout and interlinking of the roof structures, for example, is as subtle as that of the other houses. The care with which the building is placed within the landscape is equally thorough (the rocky outcrop not only provides an immediate and dramatic reminder of the surroundings, it also conveniently separates the service and delivery area from the main entrance). Indeed, during the construction phase, contractors were required to take every possible precaution to protect the existing

Low level gallery leading
to the changing rooms

Ladies' changing rooms (opposite) and overhead lighting in the men's changing rooms

landscape, in keeping with architectural principles of Sperone. The two terraces of the restaurant repeat a theme common at Sperone—a view over the sea and the *maquis*. The layout of the rooms is simple but effective: since the north-east corner gets the least amount of sunlight, it made sense to put the changing rooms there; the light increases as you penetrate further into the building. Just as the Club House links the developments of the domain, so it may be considered the crowning success of the GEA architects, given how well integrated it is into the domain as a whole.

PIANTARELLA

Walkways and stairways
leading to the apartments
at the Hameau

THE PIANTARELLA SECTOR

Construction of this last sector of the Sperone development began in 1992. To describe this section, I can do no better than to reproduce the words of Bruno Allais, the architect responsible for construction at Sperone for the past ten years. He is also responsible for the development of Piantarella, and is its best spokesman. The Sperone programme, as well as the on-site plan, was developed in 1985 and received preliminary authorizations in 1986 (*ouverture à l'urbanisation* in 1986 and *lotissement primaire* in 1987).

The initial phase of the project (1987-1990) involved the construction of residential allotments. The economic role of this development was to generate a pool of wealthy residents who would primarily reside at Sperone during the summer months.

The second phase concerned the creation of the golf course (1989-1991), which provided a new source of year-round economic activity to the area. It was designed to create an unconstructed zone amid the housing and to create an efficient fire-break.

The third phase of the programme consists of the development of the Piantarella sector, which will include facilities complementary to those constructed earlier. These include a hotel for short-term visits and conferences, apartments for short and medium-length stays staggered throughout the year, and residential allotments.

Each of these phases is an essential component of the Sperone plan; none can be eliminated without jeopardizing the overall development. All that remains is the completion of the final phase, which is Piantarella.

SITE DESCRIPTION

The site consists of a series of basins that lie 50 to 115 feet above the lagoon of Piantarella, itself separated from the sea by a narrow sand-

A house overlooking the Hameau

Axonometric perspective at Piantarella

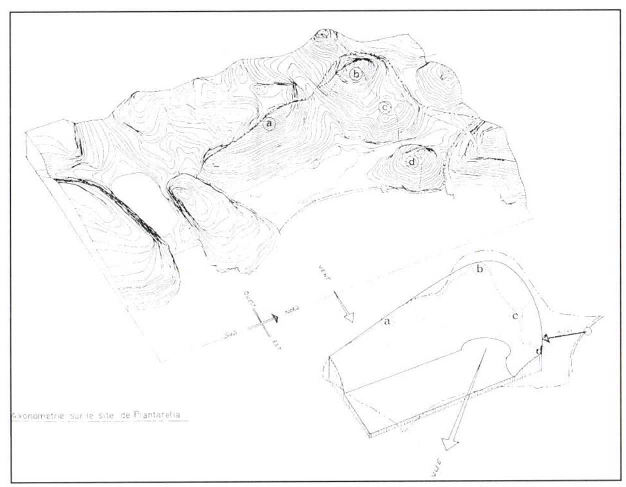

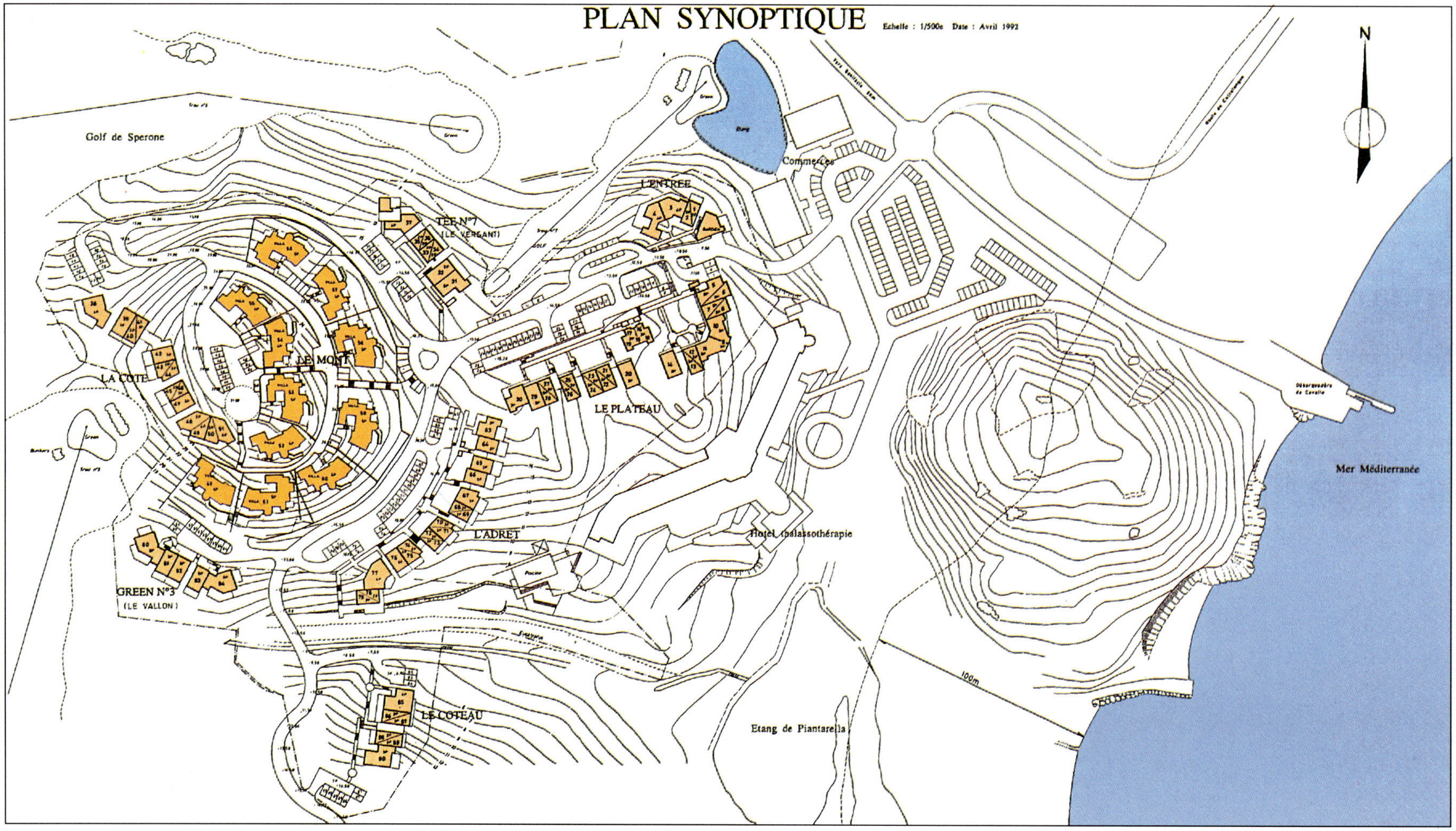

General lay-out

bar. The setting is a determining factor in the design of this protected and contained sector. The site can be reached directly from a service road and contains all the necessary conditions for a higher-density development at Sperone.

SITE LAYOUT

Hotel. The hotel, located at the entrance to the access road, is built against the hill on which the Hameau is constructed. The facade repeats many of the stylistic elements of the Hameau, underscoring its appearance as a substructure to the Hameau. The building faces out to sea—in the foreground is the lagoon of Piantarella; beyond lie the island of Piana and the Lavezzi archipelago. The hotel will be a wood-sided concrete structure, while the lower level will have a stone cladding.

The hotel will be operated by a hotel chain. The current tourist demand for hotels is essentially concentrated in July and August, making year-round operation unrealistic. Furthermore, this would place this establishment in direct competition with the existing hotel infrastructure in the region. The solution was to find an operator who could draw on its own international network to bring in business throughout the year. Various hotel chains have been contacted; the major concern is to create a high-quality hotel with conference and thalassotherapy facilities.

The Hameau. This project is already underway—the first section of twenty-six apartments (of a total of eighty) was delivered in 1993.

The overall plan of the Hameau consists of a main block of apartments situated on the plateau. A series of smaller buildings was built on a circular plan at the foot of the hill overlooking the site. Houses will be constructed on this hill up to the summit, recreating the same skyline as in many Corsican villages.

It was difficult to adapt the experience gained from designing individual villas of Spe-

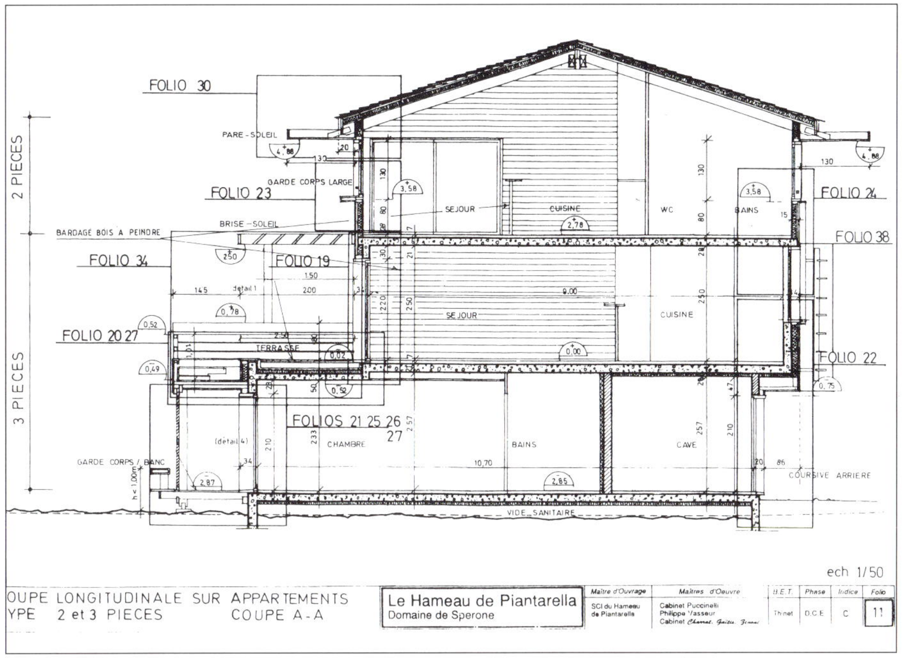

Cross-section of a building at the Hameau

An apartment at Piantarella

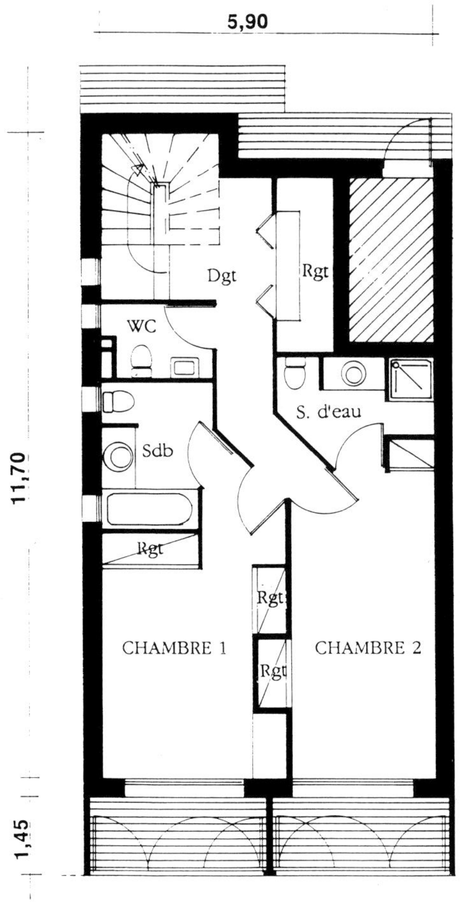

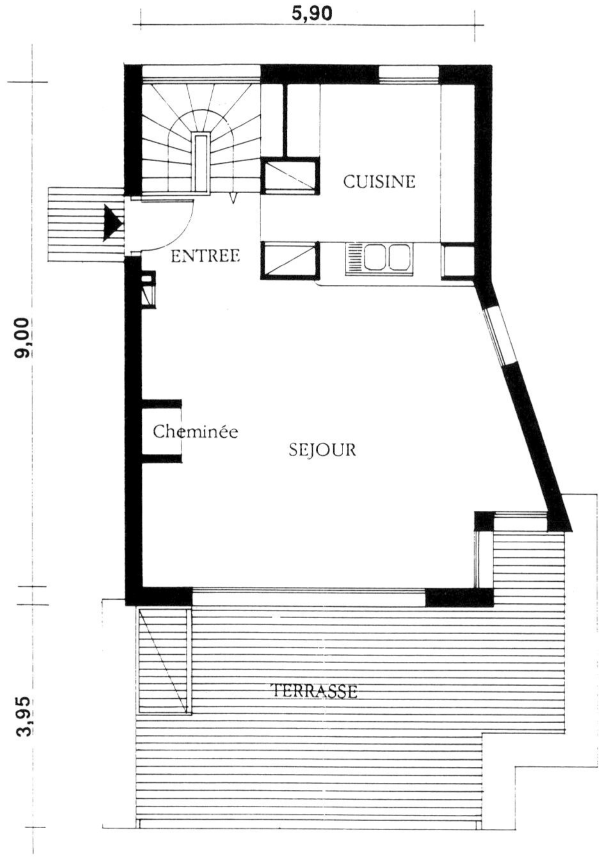

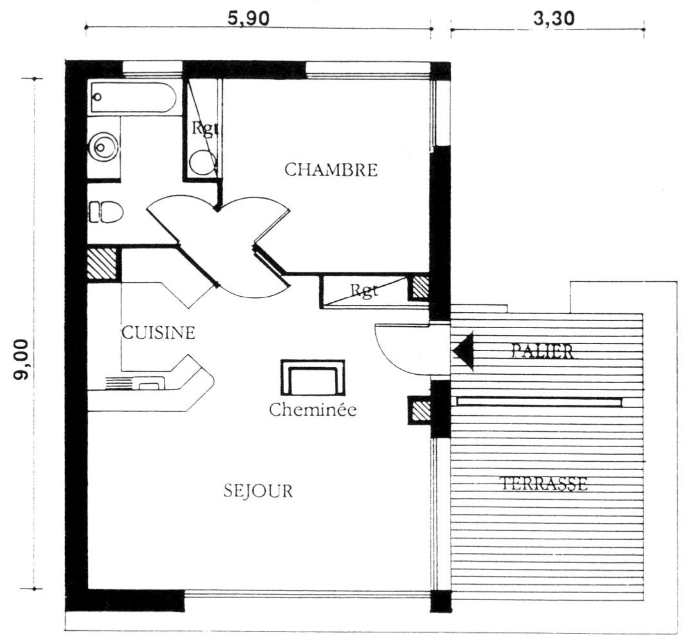

Plans of a 2- room apartment (opposite) and of a 3- room duplex apartment (above) at the Hameau

rone to a collective residence. The same principles were used as guidelines, however, and the use of wood creates a continuity in the architectural vocabulary of Sperone.

None of the buildings is higher than three storeys; they all contain spacious one- to three-room apartments. The largest apartments have two levels, and the bedrooms are situated on the lower level to take advantage of the shade from the landscaping. The living rooms, all with balconies, are located on the upper level to provide the best possible views. The facades are designed so that the terraces are as independent as possible from those of neighbouring apartments. The rigorous design of the module—the facade measures twenty feet, with a depth of thirty feet on two or three levels—contrasts with the rich detail and wooden elements (such as screens and guard rails). Outside staircases with open steps lead to a network of wooden walkways that pass through the *maquis*. Spotlights built into the planking illuminate the passages at night.

The supporting structure of the buildings is made of concrete with wood siding, like that of the Club House. Wood, however, is used for the capping (facades, frames, supports), except for separating walls and division walls.

It would have been preferable to use a timber-frame structure for these buildings, which would have modified the rigidity of the outline. The reason this was not done can be explained by the requirements specified in the Documents techniques unifiés (DTU, or Official Code of Practice), with which all contractors must comply. Although it contains highly detailed rules concerning traditional construction methods, it is sadly inadequate for timber-frame construction, a technique relatively unknown in France. All public buildings such as the Club House or housing intended for sale are required to comply with the regulations established by such regulatory authorities as SOCOTEX and VERITAS. These bodies interpret these inadequate texts in an exceedingly restrictive way; unfortunately, creativity and innovation are stifled.

Furthermore, there were not enough qualified local builders on the island to undertake a project of this scale. A hybrid solution using concrete and wood was therefore adopted.

SUBDIVISION ON THE PIANTARELLA HILLSIDE

The northern area located at the entrance to the Piantarella section was selected as the site for the high-density section of the development (the hotel and the Hameau). Farther to the south, the slope along the lagoon of Piantarella is bordered to the west by a series of ridges that drop to the south. A small valley separates it from the heavily wooded plateau, where Roman ruins are being excavated.

This final phase in the Sperone development was based on the same principles as those governing the Ciappili design—a well-defined planning and architectural scheme that would be carried out by the group itself. Iwona Buczkowska was given the responsibility of the overall design, and she proposed a grouping of fifteen luxury villas. Unfortunately, due to economic reasons, the group was forced to abandon this concept in favour of a subdivision with ten lots. The same guiding principles were used, but the project had more restrictions due to the proximity of the archaeological site, which required working in close collaboration with the *Architecte des Bâtiments de France*.

A preliminary survey for the building layout suggested the following guidelines:

The architecture should be linear and should not exceed the ridge line. It should follow the topology, and the building density should gradually diminish towards the south, until there is nothing but natural vegetation.

The design of the villas was entrusted to GEA because of the sensitivity of the area, the need to harmonize with the rest of the development, and the strict regulations concerning this small development. The subdivision has received the necessary permits, and lots are being sold; the first villas should be completed in 1996.

LAGOON OF PIANTARELLA

Numerous surveys have been made of this lagoon over the last twenty years. The most detailed of these surveys, an environmental impact study, was conducted by IARE (M. Frizoni) on the group's request.

The study reveals that the lagoon is in poor condition; indeed, it is close to disappearing.

There is little of interest in the way of plant and animal life, particularly in comparison to the remarkable Lake Sperone. It is, however, an important element in this series of lagoons on the eastern coast.

Environmental agencies wish to preserve this series of small lagoons and are hostile to any development that would include leisure facilities, especially one that transformed the lagoon into a large swimming pool.

The city council of Bonifacio, in cooperation with the environmental and prefectural services, has requested that the promoter determine the ground rules for developing the lagoon. These principles must take into account the problems—and possibilities—of an intelligent cohabitation that could reconcile the natural area with the restrictions of sensible urban development.

The extremely competent IARE and AGENC were asked to help define the basic principles of a plan that would integrate natural methods, while refusing sophisticated gimmickry or absurd financial solutions.

The findings of this survey were incorporated into Bonifacio's plan d'occupation des sols (zoning plan). The promoter has adopted these guidelines for the hotel development, which will be subject to monitoring by the environmental agencies responsible for carrying out periodic surveys of the ecosystem.

LOOKING TO THE FUTURE

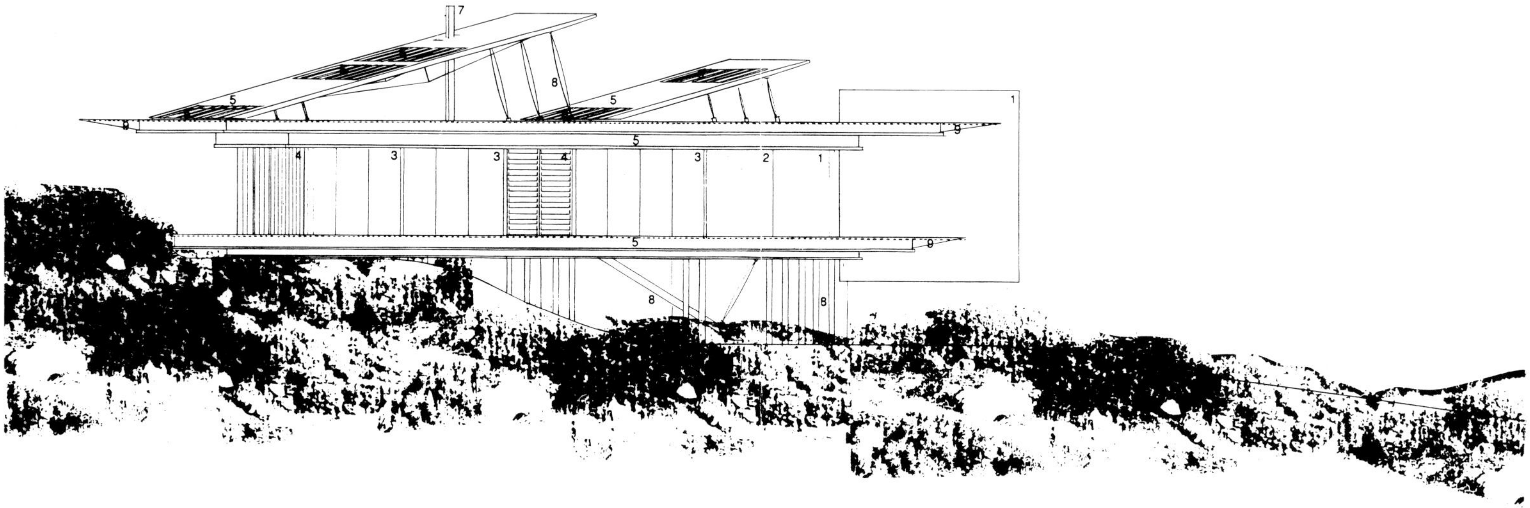

A Jean Nouvel project for a villa at Sperone

The architectural vocabulary at Sperone, developed largely by GEA, is perhaps best described as a series of small delights. As the illustrations in these pages show, the years of experience of working on the site with the contractors Italo and Longo have created the opportunity to develop a wide range of solutions to similar problems—elements contributing to these solutions include door frames, wall panels, decks, roof trusses, beams and wood-frames, staircases and benches.

The key to understanding the architecture of Sperone lies in the use of wood, which is unusual in Europe. Wood is widely used in the United States, where it is a plentiful resource. In the nineteenth century, it was even used extensively to construct railway bridges and other large engineering projects. In Europe, however, with the exception of the Scandinavian countries, wood is rarely adopted as a construction material.

Certain owners have been so impressed by this development that they have consulted architects other than those at GEA, provided that the overall guidelines set forth by GEA are scrupulously respected, particularly with regard to the building materials. The most striking example of this is architect Francis Chapus' house, built for his personal use, which incorporates an interior patio of Spanish/Moorish inspiration.

Other examples include the second Séguéla house—designed by Jean-François Bodin—the house constructed by Sir Norman Foster, as well as several designs by Jean Nouvel. The house designed by Jean Nouvel and illustrated in this book remains unfinished. He drew on the motif of an aircraft carrier as inspiration for this villa at Falatte. Two ramps lead from the fully glassed-in floor to an immense deck, on which horizontal nets serve as railings. This idea links the wood-frame construction at Sperone to the traditions of naval architecture.

It is always interesting to see how a "high-tech" architect such as Sir Norman Foster will

The Jean-François Bodin design for the Séguéla house

The house designed at Sperone by Sir Norman Foster

use a new material. Foster and his colleagues took up the challenge of wood with their usual enthusiasm. The house seems to be constructed below a ramp, and the roof ridge appears to emerge from the *maquis*, ending with a sort of triumphal arch that overlooks the 33-foot-high glass wall forming the façade. This house, so different from all the others, may appear to be provocative, but I believe that in time, it will be integrated into the environment, just like the nearby houses. Although the proximity of the golf course to the glass façade has already been the subject of amused speculation in architectural reviews, Sir Norman Foster's contribution only adds to the success of the overall development.

Iwona Buczkowska's remarkable project for a complex of 18 villas at Piantarella, all variations on the same theme, had to be abandonned for economic reasons. According to the architect, "this project was inspired from lighthouses, the towers of San Giminiano and the Genoese towers. The central section is the highest part of the house, and provides the best view of the sea. In time, once the *maquis* has reconquered the site, only the tops of the houses will be visible. They will mark the slope of the hillside, just as a lighthouse delimits the entrance to a port."

The arrival of new architects does not in any way suggest that the GEA team—which has done such excellent work on the domain—have exhausted their resources. It is, rather, proof that the Sperone style is so well established that it has become a working model for other designers. Even in this last phase, the name of Sperone continues to offer a challenge and a new vision of Mediterranean architecture.

Model for a villa at Piantarella by the architect Iwona Buczkowska. Curved structures such as those create spectacular interiors, that recall the original helical plan for Ciappili

Appendix 1:
Notes by the architects of GEA

ARCHITECTURE AND BUILDING TECHNIQUES

MATERIAL SELECTED: WOOD

Wood is used as a framing material on the outside (red cedar siding on the vertical sections, cedar shakes for the roofs, planks of red cedar for the terraces), the inside (siding and floors), and for built-in elements (libraries, bars and benches) and furniture (tables, chairs, armchairs and beds).

REASONS FOR THIS DECISION

1. *Structural qualities*: wood is light, versatile (used for pillaring, cantilevers, large spans to allow wide openings, suitable for steep slopes, it preserves existing environment). It is easy to handle, so that heavy hoisting equipment is not necessary. This provides the possibility of creating a greater variety of volumes, openings and layouts. Furthermore, the "legibility" of wood elements creates an integrated aesthetic.

2. *Insulating qualities*: wood is a good insulator against cold and heat (ventilated external "skin").

3. *Mechanical qualities*: the overhangs of a beam alleviate its flexion between two supports; a larger span can therefore be achieved.

4. *Wood is easy to work with, and is a noble, attractive material*: different woods have a different appearance and feel. There is a large variety of species: hardwood, softwood, dense wood. Wood comes in many different colours and grains: light, red, dark and black. It can be finished in various ways: planed, sanded or rough. It has good insulating qualities and is pleasant and sensual to live around (good for bare feet). Added to this is the sentimental aspect of wood as a living material—a tree, symbol of life. This material, used in construction for centuries, is deeply anchored in our unconscious and is linked to our earliest memories. The use of wood was necessary as a return to our roots, and to create the framework for a "free" lifestyle, in harmony with the elements, nature and the environment.

VARIOUS TECHNIQUES

CIAPPILI (steeply sloped terrain)

Two construction "blocks" linked by elevated terraces. Living area: raised on pillars, using supporting post-and-beam construction with angle ties and wind bracing so that wide openings could be made. Bedroom area: reinforced concrete or concrete-block foundations with platform framing and small openings.

SPERONE (section with a steep slope)

Pillaring to conform with the lay of the land. Post-and-beam construction. Wind bracing: tie beams and angle braces. Balloon-frame system on platform.

SPERONE AND FALATTE (low-pitched slope)

Balloon-frame platform on low concrete-block walls or joist and transom flooring.

CLADDING

Red cedar siding (heat protection to prevent the outside walls from heating up). Horizontal siding for linear, horizontal houses that are set within the landscape; vertical siding for vertical housing.

We felt that roofs were "philosophically" essential to the concept of "shelter" and remain the simplest and most efficient protection against the elements.

CIAPPILI

The roofs, all oriented in the same direction to protect the houses from the prevailing westerly winds, impart an architectural unity to the village. The architectural forms are a consequence of this layout. as, for example, in floor plans that radiate out from a vertical volume along the roof line. Large roof over-hangs can be designed with timber-frame construction (rafters/ decking with a span less than six feet), which provide protection from the sun, wind and rain (gutters are therefore not necessary).

SPERONE – FALATTE

Different roof slopes were used in conjunction with a general horizontality befitting the landscape.

Large roof overhangs, often extended by porches, or galleries and verandahs.

Exceptions: The "modernist" design of the Feldman and Roux houses; the "cubist" design of the Du Payrat and Pommereau houses (pavilioned roof delimiting the main areas).

Terrace roofs: accessible as both a solarium and summer house. An open red-cedar deck over a wood structure creates a perfectly sealed terrace.

FRAMEWORK

Open-beams, such as the ribs of the roof structure, make the construction more "legible"; it is easier to understand and appreciate.

A wide range of technical solutions and shapes were used: straight or radiating frames, king posts or more complicated trusses, tie beams and so forth.

ADDITIONAL ELEMENTS

The large openings were protected from the sun by directional red-cedar sun screens, which also provided an additional depth to the walls. Bow and oriel windows. Kiosks: outside living areas and shelters for meals and pool houses.

OPENINGS

Holes in the walls frame the landscape while protecting private areas in exposed walls from wind and intrusions. Glass walls retract into the walls or slide; door thresholds are built into the wooden floors; use of wooden lintels: solid or composite beams. Technical solutions were adapted to each problem: half-timbered construction, sliding door rails extending outside the house.

ORIELS

These windows provide a "directional" view (see the Bériot staircase) or panoramic views (three-sided bow windows), and add depth to walls and an undulating aspect to outside walls, without interfering with the roof lines.

TERRACES – OUTSIDE SPACES

A beautiful natural environment (vegetation and rocks), Mediterranean climate and exceptional views all call for the creation of outside living areas as extensions to the interior spaces. They must, however, preserve the natural vegetation and be designed in accordance with the topography and rocks, providing protection from the wind and sun. These spaces had to adapt to the slopes, while remaining private.

Terraces: a wide variety of solutions are possible using wood as the primary material: wooden decks that enclose or bypass the natural vegetation and rocks; terraces that project into space, "floating" over the vegetation; decks created in enclosed volumes or protected by low wooden walls (wind-breaks or screens); and pergolas that filter the sun.

INSULATION

Thermal: wood, rock wool, ventilated partition walls, roof overhangs.

Sound-proofing: this was achieved through the layout of the living spaces (day/night, intimate/collective); and the use of walls, including concrete-blocks between bedrooms and separate wood partition walls.

PRIVATE AREAS/OPEN SPACES–TRANSITIONS

The immediate environment is set off by pillaring, by the layout of volumes along the differing levels, and by the terraces.

The first houses at Ciappili were built by a company from Gap, which specializes in timber-frame construction. A local company (SIC, owned by Longo and Italo) was then trained to use these techniques for the construction of the Ikam house at Ciappili. GEA provided all the technical specifications, including the nailing diagrams, which are still used as a reference today. Since then, the company has added several improvements (waterproofing, insulation, ventilation, window frames). The architecture, which is closely linked to the topography, evolved as construction progressed. Changes to the project conception (year-round occupation, comfort) also largely contributed to improvements in the services provided (particularly since the Gallais house).

The joining techniques, however, have remained the same. This company, trained by GEA, has been able to develop wood-frame structures far beyond the level of the American model.

Admittedly, the conditions governing this development were not the same as those prevailing in America, where wood-frame houses are a readily available product and houses are enlarged, remodeled and transformed with each new generation or transfer of ownership. In France, due to the prevailing masonry construction techniques and regulations, the houses are built to last.

Appendix 2: Technical developments Role of the company

The first houses had unpainted, unstained siding, which does not affect the quality of the house if wood is protected by overhangs and waterproofing. Stain was first used at Sperone (notably for the Roux house). It protects the wood and creates a coherent colour, while leaving the wooden structure visible; however, the stain must be reapplied approximately every five years.

The opaque paint currently in use in the United States offers a greater protection and has appeared on some of the more recent houses at Sperone. There is a greater variety of colours, but it is at the expense of the material's integrity.

The techniques used for the acoustic insulation of the timber-frame structures are fairly sophisticated and costly. At Sperone, concrete is used as a supplementary material to improve the acoustic comfort (slabs and cross walls). Aluminium doors and windows: this material provides a better seal than wood, the elements are lightweight, and they exist in a wide range of colours. This material has therefore become the ideal counterpart to wood for exterior doors and windows.

VARIOUS WOODS USED

Only red cedar is used for the outside siding, but the framing material may be red cedar, hemlock or pine. The Lariccio pine (or Corsican pine) is not used because, though a high-quality wood, its current processing methods (cutting, storage, working and treatment) are not suitable for timber-frame construction.

Printed in October 1996
by Milanostampa,
Farigliano, Italy